W9-BYV-555

PUPPY
savvy

The Pocket Guide to Raising Your
Dog Without Going Bonkers

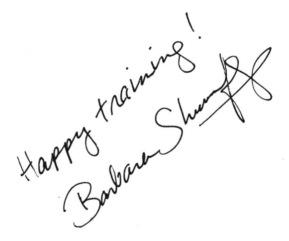

Happy training!
Barbara Shumannfang

PUPPY
savvy

The Pocket Guide to Raising Your Dog Without Going Bonkers

Barbara Shumannfang

ISBN 978-1-300-26879-6

Cover design by Barbara Shumannfang.

Author photo by Kristen Beck.

Also by Barbara Shumannfang

Happy Kids, Happy Dogs:
Building a Friendship Right From the Start

For Dave.

Preface

One day I met with a new dog-training client at her home. She had a bouncy little puppy, three young children, and a list of things that weren't going so well. The puppy wouldn't poop in the area of the yard they wanted, he grabbed and tugged on his leash instead of walking along, he screeched to high heaven in his crate and, last but not least, he bit the kids' hands and arms if they so much as thought about moving them. She was rethinking the wisdom of their choice to get a puppy. Who could blame her?

We dove in and she and the kids did a fantastic job during the appointment. The puppy responded beautifully and started behaving better right before our very eyes. (The magic of dog training never ceases to amaze me. I felt compelled to tell the woman that I had not slipped the little whippersnapper $5 to get him to pipe down.) The relief in the air was palpable; it was all going to be okay. On my way out the door, she looked at me with moist eyes and said, "May I give you a hug?"

I was very touched by that, and I also wished I could find some way to keep puppy raising from being so emotionally taxing. I myself have looked at my puppy with desperation, stood at the kitchen sink and cried, and laughed myself silly at his antics, all before lunchtime. And that's despite thirteen years of practice with clients' dogs and my own plus working with some of the best dog trainers in the field. All I can tell you is that feeling frustrated does not mean you're a mess. It means it's a big undertaking, you're trying hard, you're probably sleep-deprived from housetraining, and your puppy is lucky you care enough to get a little worked up now and then.

Just the same, the point is not to see how overwhelmed you can get, so all the tips I gave that client are in this book, along with many others I have used over the years. I have learned valuable lessons from puppies who were so mellow they fell asleep during the appointment, and from others who had such abnormal aggression problems the clients were considering euthanasia. By no means do you have to use all of this information. Just pick and choose what works best for you. Do your best given your schedule, values and priorities, and give yourself a break. You know best what you need.

You also know your puppy better than anyone. As you have probably figured out, your puppy has unique preferences, quirks and abilities. Part of the reason I wrote this book is to invite you to appreciate your dog as a thinking, feeling individual. My hope is that will make it easier to work with him rather than to battle against him, and to identify with what your puppy is going through. My guess is that you have deep reserves of compassion and respect for others. Learning to live with your puppy is a great opportunity to tap into those and model them for others, including kids.

As they say, it takes a village, and in addition to training strategies your puppy also needs top-notch veterinary care. Veterinarians tell me that the most common questions they get during puppy wellness appointments are training-related. So, my additional hope for this book is that it will provide answers to your questions about puppy training topics such as socialization, housetraining, chewing and fetch so that you and your veterinarian will have more time to focus on disease prevention and how best to care for your pup. Of course your veterinarian is also a great source of referrals to local dog trainers. Heck, you can create a whole team of helpers for your puppy (maybe even get matching jerseys).

As you may have discovered by now with your pup, dogs tend not to read the same books we do or follow the formula we intend. Maybe you are wondering how the other puppies in class are practically ready for college compared to your puppy. Maybe you are stumped as to why your puppy does the things he does, despite your efforts. Maybe you are wondering if it is normal to feel so exhausted when having a puppy was supposed to be fun. I hope this book helps you, your puppy and your veterinarian. Remember, it's all going to be okay.

Acknowledgements

I am so grateful for all the help I had creating this book. I thank my friends and fellow dog lovers Gita Gulati-Partee and Wendy Wahman who gave helpful comments on early drafts and who buoyed me with their enthusiasm. Emma Skurnick helped keep me on schedule and gave me well-timed high fives. I thank the DogPros for their camaraderie and for sharing their boundless dog training expertise. I offer huge thanks to Drs. Alison Klaitman and Suzanne Hughes for lending their veterinary expertise to this book. They have also helped me immeasurably with my own puppies and as a dog trainer. Virginia Hoffmann and Janice Triptow, priceless friends and dog trainers extraordinaire, challenged and supported me, and made me laugh along the way. Thanks to Cathy Whitt for freeing the book of typos, to the crackerjack formatting team at Lulu, and to Kristen Beck for creating the author photo despite the mud and camera-shy dogs. Thanks to Chris O'Connor for understanding the agony and the ecstasy of dogs and for helping me maintain my sense of humor. I am grateful to Alison Klaitman, Lee Newlin and Tina Fang for believing in me and making this book adventure richer, more fun, and more possible.

I am deeply honored to have shared in the puppy training of my clients' dogs. I thank them for inviting me into their lives to experience their very personal hurdles and triumphs. They and their dogs have taught me so much about life, relationships, loss and love.

I am awfully glad my dogs can't read. I wouldn't know how to begin to thank them.

Contents

Part I
How to Be Puppy Savvy

Chapter 1

Treat Yourself To A Dream Puppy: No Bribes, No Bullying

If you've owned a dog before or know someone with a dog, you know that there are many differing opinions on how to best teach a puppy what you want him to learn. How can you be sure which approach is right for your pup? This guide will give you the state-of-the art, most effective approach. Plus, as an added bonus, you will get tips that professionals use to customize training according to a puppy's personality. Who doesn't like a bonus?

As you know, every professional field evolves as knowledge advances. For example, your veterinarian does not practice like she did ten years ago. She uses improvements in the field, like pain medicine, to take even better care of your dog. Veterinarians now know that preventing and controlling pain are important for your dog's well being.

The same is true of the field of professional dog training. There are better techniques now than were available ten years ago. You will be able to do an even better job of training and communicating with your puppy while taking into account both your goals and your dog's well being.

For example, dogs thrive when they have clear boundaries and routines established for them by their people. The ability of dogs to learn these routines means they get to go more places, be a part of the family, and stay in their homes for life. When these boundaries are established through intimidation or physical force, however, there is unintended fallout. Using modern dog training, you will be able to avoid the use or threat of force and still teach your puppy boundaries and rules through rewards. Pretty neat, huh?

When applied correctly, reward-based training works so well that it is almost mind-boggling. Nowadays police dogs, search and rescue dogs, and dogs at the highest level of dog sports are trained this way. Families across the world are catching on to this effective way to get the training results they want for a well-mannered companion dog.

The key is to know the difference between bribes and rewards. While some people coax a dog with treats or toys, I am sorry to say that approach rarely yields reliable results. (Picture yourself running through your neighborhood in your pajamas, a slice of deli meat flapping in your hand, as you frantically call your dog, who is cruising around at warp speed. Nightmare!) As you can imagine, an exciting distraction like another dog or a visitor to your home would be enough to make bribe-based training fail.

What *does* produce reliable results is the strategic application of rewards. Actions that are rewarded become stronger, more reliable, more intense, and harder to break down, even in the face of distractions. This book will reveal many of the ways you might have inadvertently rewarded your puppy for things you didn't actually want repeated, and how you can instead harness the power of rewards to build great habits in your puppy. It is important to give your puppy a fair chance to succeed and then reward him after he has behaved well. The secret is to learn what is rewarding to your puppy and to be quick to provide the reward as a surprise for behavior you like. Your puppy then will then become highly motivated to repeat the behaviors you want, without being dependent on the lure of treats or toys.

It's not hard; my reward-based training colleagues and I teach people (including children) to do it all the time. And it is impressive to see the results when it is done well. (Picture yourself standing on your doorstep in your pajamas, coffee in hand as your dog brings you the morning paper. Dreamy!)

If you are like most people with a new puppy, you would like your pup to learn house rules, be polite with people and other pets, leave your possessions alone, play appropriately, potty only outdoors, walk nicely on leash, respond to you when you need him to come to you, and settle down without a fuss. Using this guide is the first step toward meeting those goals so that you can enjoy life together.

And then there's the bonus: For most of the training tips, you'll learn how to adapt them if your puppy's personality is on the bold side or if he is more on the bashful side. More on that in the following pages.

Let's get started!

Chapter 2

How Your Puppy Is Just Like An Alligator

Imagine that you and your family have decided to adopt a pet alligator. First you would find out a little about alligators, then you'd visit ReptileFinder online to look at photos and pick the cutest one, and finally you'd bring the little dickens home.

Soon the alligator would start exhibiting her normal behaviors. She would slip into the goldfish pond in your garden and wreak havoc (pretend you have a goldfish pond). She would hide under the couch to take a nap, ripping the underside of the upholstery with her pointy back. She would open her huge mouth, holding it wide in a toothy threat display because you approached her too fast. The sight of her gaping, massive jaws would probably scare the you-know-what out of you.

Obviously you would not say to yourself, "This is a naughty alligator! I need to learn how to discipline her!" You would think, "Well, duh. Alligators need to do alligator things. I had better get a kiddie pool, a raised platform underneath which she can nap, and, to put her at ease, I need to learn to move differently around her."

But it is not so obvious with a dog who appears to be naughty. Why not? It is because, unlike with an alligator, or for that matter literally any other animal on earth, the natural histories of dogs and humans are specially intertwined. Some scientists would even say humans and dogs have co-evolved. We "get" each other in ways that no other human/non-human pair understands each other. We have emotions in common and enjoy many of the same things. Dogs can read our body language and facial expressions, and even anticipate and fulfill our needs. It's not your imagination.

However, we tend not to return the favor by trying to understand what our dogs are feeling and what they're trying to tell us. Why? Because we are in charge, so we don't trouble ourselves with it. We generally consider dogs' needs and opinions less valuable than ours. When you think about it, that is a pretty arrogant attitude (some would call it "speciest"). That's not the kind of person most of us want to be. Golden Rule and all, if you see what I mean.

Honestly, there is no harm in giving your puppy the same consideration you would an alligator. It might even teach you and your kids something about yourselves, and about how we treat those who are similar yet different from us.

Granted, it is not always easy to live with another species. I don't blame you one bit if at times you get emotional with your puppy, or try to explain to her the rules in the way that makes sense only to a human, or feel like she should know better. We all get sucked into that, partly because of how much we have in common with dogs. The connection we have with dogs is downright amazing, but it is no wonder the lines get blurry about what we expect they should automatically know. We have given them the role of family member, fashion accessory, disposable project, worker, best friend, menu item, hero, and hat trim, just to name a few. It's confusing, to be sure. They are so like us, and at the same time we could do a lot better job of understanding and respecting our differences.

Perhaps we could meet our dogs halfway. If we make even a tiny effort to see things from their point of view, to learn to read their body language and meet their needs, I think we'll be pleasantly surprised at how much more harmonious life can be. We may even learn a thing or two from them.

Oh and the alligator thing was just a made-up analogy. I really doubt it is a good idea (or, you know, legal) to live with one.

Chapter 3

Secrets to Success from Elmo's Diner: (Hint: Take Control of Your Puppy's Coloring Book and His Pancakes)

Here in a nutshell is the secret formula to being truly puppy savvy:

a) Imagine what you wish your puppy would do.

b) Set up the situation to make that desired behavior likely, and then, when your puppy behaves as you wish,

c) Surprise! Present a reward that matters to your puppy. The behavior you reward will become a habit.

One of my favorite restaurants, Elmo's Diner in Durham, North Carolina, uses this approach to great effect (with humans, though I am sure they could teach a puppy to do anything). When you ask for a table at Elmo's, if you have children the friendly host seats you with menus, crayons, and sheets of paper with the Elmo's cartoon duck to color in (just to help you visualize it, like his cousin Donald the Elmo's duck wears no pants). The Elmo's staff thereby applies the same principles that will yield great results for you and your puppy. They a) wish young kids would color instead of whine or tear around the restaurant and b) they make this coloring behavior likelier by, right off the bat, presenting the opportunity to color in a way that makes it a special ritual (the stuff is not just sitting out on the table). Then c) Surprise! In the middle of the coloring session, they deliver the pancakes and juice the parents have ordered. The kids are invited to hang their masterpieces on the Duck Wall in the lobby or take the duck home with them. Some of the ducks are even featured on the Elmo's website Duck Gallery.

At Elmo's the whole coloring experience becomes rewarding in itself, and therefore a habit the kids want to repeat next time they come in. The Elmo's staff members don't wait to see what self-rewarding behaviors the little tykes come up with on their own and then try to get the situation under control after the fact. I have also never seen a host at Elmo's dangle a pancake in front of a child, promising they can have the treat if they'd just please behave until the food is ready. That would be bribery and it would not work, not reliably and not long-term. No, they are not desperate at Elmo's, they are geniuses of reward-based training and I love them, their food, and the peaceful dining experience I can count on.

And so it should be with your puppy. Will you let your puppy gallivant through the environment, letting his adventures and the taste of your favorite shoes be his rewards? (Yes, it is inherently rewarding for most pups to explore closets, houseplants and trash containers, to take off running outside, to pee when they really need to go, dig holes, and chase and bite at squealing kids. Whee, big fun!) Will you then unintentionally pile on more rewards, making these puppy behaviors even stronger by interacting with him ("No!" "Come back!" "Give me that!")? That is unconscious training with inadvertent rewards. These unintentional rewards are just as powerful and build habits just as well as rewards given for the puppy behaving as we'd like. Unfortunately we are then stuck trying to teach our puppies why something that feels so right to them is so "wrong" according to us. That can be a frustrating quagmire for human and puppy alike, let me tell you.

You can choose a better way. You can harness the power of rewards to your advantage and to help your puppy. You can use rewards consciously and strategically. You can use a baby gate, a crate or x-pen, an indoor leash known as a dragline and an indoor tether to keep your pup out of mischief, and always give him the equivalent of a coloring book to keep him occupied (a game or a stuffed Kong are often good options). You can get in the habit of never taking the puppy out of his crate (or off his indoor tether) without first having a specific answer to the question, "What will I give the puppy to do next that will set him up to succeed? What game, project, training session, edible toy or other 'coloring book' will I offer right off the bat?"

The answer to this question will depend on what your puppy likes, your mood, what you have time for, and even the weather. Perhaps you would like to teach the pup to play fetch or go to his spot. Maybe you would rather tether the pup with a stuffed Kong while you finish some emails. Or perhaps a puppy field trip would be a good choice to provide socialization and get you both out of the house. Simply choose from the Magic Wand strategies, Life Lessons or Training Skills described in this book. I find it helpful to write each puppy-occupying game, skill or chew toy on a small piece of paper, put all the slips of paper in a bowl near the puppy's crate, and fish one out before I release the puppy. I call this the Bowl of Happiness.

 Anytime you are about to let the puppy out of his crate or exercise pen, save your sanity and be fair to the pup by asking yourself, "After I take him out to pee, what am I going to do next with the puppy to set him up to succeed?" Always have a plan before you release the hound!

Once your puppy is engaged in the constructive activity you have offered, you have created a rewardable moment. Surprise your puppy with a reward and you have made an investment in that desirable behavior being repeated. In no time flat, your puppy is going to start choosing the behaviors you prefer, all on his own, because you have made them so rewarding. Yes, it takes work, but it is so much less exhausting than letting him run circles around you, doing myriad things you wish he wouldn't. The satisfaction that results for you will be as delicious as a stack of fluffy, maple syrup drizzled pancakes.

Remember, the reward has to matter to your puppy. What does your puppy enjoy? Sometimes it is obvious, and sometimes you'll really need to see things from your pup's perspective. Food and toys matter to most puppies and are great ways to reward them, sure, but why not be truly puppy savvy? Observe what your pup likes and then use that as a reward. For example, when your puppy has just responded to his name, surprise-reward him with a chance to play outside. When he has approached you calmly without jumping up, surprise him with a good butt scratch if he truly loves that. When he comes to you outside, run with him to explore under a bush or let him chase you all over the yard. What does he like best?

Do use treats as surprise-rewards, absolutely. And to really make the fastest progress, save yourself the most aggravation, and appreciate what matters to your puppy, set your puppy up to succeed and, after your puppy has behaved as you like, surprise him with the everyday thing he likes best.

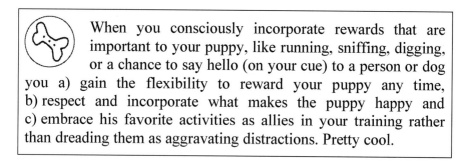

When you consciously incorporate rewards that are important to your puppy, like running, sniffing, digging, or a chance to say hello (on your cue) to a person or dog you a) gain the flexibility to reward your puppy any time, b) respect and incorporate what makes the puppy happy and c) embrace his favorite activities as allies in your training rather than dreading them as aggravating distractions. Pretty cool.

Chapter 4

Bold or Bashful?

While each of us can have bold or bashful moments, some of us have personalities that we would describe as overall bold or generally bashful. The same is true for dogs. It does not matter what size, breed or age the puppy is, he likely has a personality tendency one way or the other. Bold and bashful are not euphemisms for "aggressive" and "fearful" (any puppy can have a moment in which he displays aggressive or fearful behavior). Bold and bashful are also not set-in-stone labels; rather they indicate a personality tendency.

Whether bold or bashful, one is not better than the other. The reason it helps to be aware of your pup's personality tendency is that having that awareness will lead you to a training approach that is faster, more effective and less work for you. Besides, the more you get to know your pup as an individual, the more you will understand and appreciate him.

The training techniques in this guide will work whether your puppy is bold, bashful, or middle of the road. Each section will have special tips to allow you to progress faster or troubleshoot better depending on whether your pup is bold or bashful. Personally, I never refuse a special tip.

You probably already have a sense of whether your pup is especially bold or tends to be bashful. That's because there are behaviors (actions the puppy does) and body postures that tell you how the pup is feeling, and you have probably picked up on those. Here are some typical ones:

Bold behavior: walking right up to a stranger without hesitation, maybe even looking right into the person's face

Bold body language: head held up, body aligned head-on to the person, perhaps even with the tail in a high position relative to his back

Bashful behavior: hesitating to approach a stranger, perhaps looking down or away as they approach

Bashful body language: head or tail held low, body curved or angled to the person

Instead of being judgmental about this (by assuming that one way to act or feel is better than another) just be aware of your puppy's tendency, and build on strengths he has. As we know from our own lives and interactions with others, sometimes it really comes in handy to be bold, and sometimes it works out much better to be bashful. The point is to appreciate your puppy and work with his or her tendencies instead of against them.

Chapter 5

The Magic Wand: Quick Reference Chart To Fix The World's Most Annoying Puppy Behaviors

The Magic Wand chart will allow you to choose your preferred solution for bothersome behaviors your puppy does, from very basic Quick Fixes up to fancy Extra Slick solutions. You may want a Quick Fix for some or all of these issues, you may decide to Make it Stick on others, and you may want just a few of the Extra Slick solutions. It is completely up to you and what you have the time and desire to accomplish. Each column builds on the previous; you won't get good results if you skip any.

These solutions make use of the following strategies:

- Prevent rehearsal of actions you don't want to become habits.
- Teach and reward actions you do want to become your puppy's habits.
- Try to see things from your puppy's point of view. He is not a person so he will do things that make sense from a puppy perspective. Your job is to think ahead (or just use the chart) to provide something he finds satisfying in order to prevent the thing you find annoying.

Extra Slick Training: Is It for You?

Aiming for the Extra Slick training is more about commitment than difficulty level. Truly, anyone can do the Extra Slick training if they want to try it, and they have done the previous columns. It is just a few more minutes a day of effort and consistency on your part.

In other words, if you are a micromanaging control freak such as myself, you will experience great pleasure in being able to quietly ask your puppy to lie down on his place instead of bothering your dinner guests. Everyone will admire your puppy for the genius that he is, and you might even get on the Ellen show. Or you can just do the Quick Fix and get on with your life. Granted, that won't get you on the Ellen show, but to be realistic, that was unlikely anyway.

Achieving the Extra Slick training shows really stellar communication between you and your puppy, and an extra effort on your part to give your pup some skills and language that will allow you to function as a team and with less stress for both of you. Plus, I will send you a Gold Star (I don't kid about Gold Stars).

When It Is Time To Say "No" Or Swat Your Puppy

What if your puppy makes his way to the electrical cord, laundry basket, fabulous new stilettos, carpet fringe, your child's favorite toy or a snack she is holding? Obviously there is no point in yelling at, scolding, grabbing or striking your puppy who is a baby and doesn't know how to live with humans. Referring to hitting as "cuffing under the chin" or "rapping on the nose" doesn't change the fact that it's hitting. There is no need to hit your puppy. Besides being unfair and ineffective, it may cause problems with aggression, fear of human hands, or problems with your children if they see you do it. The good news is that there is no need to physically intimidate your pooch.

If you miss a prevention opportunity and your pup is engaged in something you don't want to become a habit, neutrally remove the pup from the situation (to prevent further reward from the activity) by guiding him with his dragline, picking him up, or interrupting him by clapping your hands or gasping dramatically. Then confine him with a chewy (to prevent barking) until you can clean up and regroup.

Some people like to say "no." However, the puppy has no idea what that means. Meanwhile the human gets sucked into feeling they've communicated something meaningful. The next steps are usually nagging and frustration when the puppy inevitably repeats the undesirable behavior.

Next time, proactively choose and reward habits from the chart below *before* he has a chance to get into mischief. Personally, I would go nuts if I had to teach my puppy every cotton pickin' thing he should not do in life (the list is infinite, it would be exhausting). A few setbacks are normal, but choosing and rewarding behavior you like should be your goal. Create discipline and good habits by keeping your pup occupied with rewarding activities that are human-approved, and by the time he's hitting adolescence in a few months he'll be well on his way to behaving as you like. It is crazy effective.

When you see the pup headed for mischief, step on and reach for the end of the dragline furthest from the puppy. Then move in the opposite direction from the pup. The line joins the two of you, so he will follow you. Then change the subject, so to speak, by getting him involved in an appropriate activity.

The Magic Of Tethering With A Food Puzzle

A dragline is a lightweight 6-foot line or leash your puppy will wear on his flat collar and drag around behind him that you can use to reel him in when necessary. It's a great tool to prevent bad habits during your puppy's first couple of weeks. An indoor tether is easily fashioned from the pup's dragline by tying the dragline to a piece of furniture. This limits your puppy's ability to choose habits you don't like and conditions him to lie quietly with a chew toy. You'll likely need to use it only for a month or two, then gradually wean off it by providing just the chew toy. Indoor tethering is only for when you are in the same room with the puppy (tether the pup to your belt loop if you'll be going in and out of the room), always involves an engrossing chew toy, and is not a good choice if kids or other pets are free to encroach on the pup's space.

The Magic Wand

Puppy Problem	Quick Fix	Make it Stick	Extra Slick
Taking or chewing your stuff	Crate, tether, or otherwise confine your pup when not directly interacting with him. Provide and rotate appropriate chew-outlets and provide plenty of exercise.	Engage your pup in interesting games instead of letting him wander loose in search of his own adventure. Try: find it, hide-n-seek, come, down-stay, tricks and go to your place.	Teach your pup to automatically retrieve to you interesting things he finds.
Trying to get on furniture	Tether pup nearby with edible chew toy. When not home, confine away from furniture.	Body block sofa like soccer goalie to prevent getting on furniture. Reward with treats for lying elsewhere.	Teach pup to go to his place on cue. If desired, teach pup to get on only certain furniture, on cue.
Biting hands when you try to pet	Before petting puppy, offer plush toy twice size of his mouth, or feed treats while petting. No rough play or touch, by anyone.	Complete the body handling exercises and the Weekly Once Over to help him love restraint and touch.	Teach Nose Touch to hand so pup has calm association with hands and touches them with a closed mouth.

Puppy Problem	Quick Fix	Make it Stick	Extra Slick
Jumping up on people	Use leash (can stand on it), dragline (step on it) or baby gate to prevent pup from launching himself on you or visitors. Tiny dog? Pick him up before he has the chance to jump.	Approach when pup has all fours on floor, retreat if paws lift. Feed treats at knee level for all approaches. Teach pup Nose Touch to hands as default greeting behavior.	Teach pup to sit instead. Use Animal Game (see Jumping Up section) and high value rewards.
Peeing or pooping indoors	Take pup out every 30 minutes and crate when not directly interacting with pup. Feed on schedule (leave food out no longer than 10 minutes).	Reward pup each time he eliminates outdoors. Feed a treat right then and there, and then offer a walk or playtime.	Keep a log to record when, where and what puppy eliminated and who was in charge of taking him out. This will reveal the missing link.
Ignoring you outside	Use a leash, long line or fence for your pup's safety, and to keep your puppy from disturbing others or their property.	Reward all voluntary eye contact with favorite food tidbits. Cue to "go sniff" the environment as a reward for doing a sit or nose touch.	Teach puppy to return to you when you call his name, even under distraction. Add distractions indoors first, using outrageous rewards.
Biting leash or your clothes	Dangle rope toy beside you as you walk *before* pup starts biting. If bites, gently guide leash motionless toward sky (all four puppy feet must stay on ground!) and wait for release. Trade clothes/leash for treat. Be ready to offer rope toy.	Teach pup to sit for a treat every few steps as you walk. Vary rewards: toss treat behind you, drag toy erratically on ground, cue Nose Touch.	Teach puppy to retrieve/release things to you on cue (in this case his leash; see Fetch section).
Not interested in training treats	Train at mealtime using dog food in place of treats. Follow all treat delivery with something pup likes better (i.e. chase game).	Train new things in distraction-free environment only, using highly tasty treats like cut up Tofu Pups.	Once new skill is strong, use non-food rewards like release to favorite toy, sniff opportunity or chase game to maintain the skill.

Puppy Problem	Quick Fix	Make it Stick	Extra Slick
Straining on the leash or sitting and not budging	Use well-fitted Sensation brand or other front attachment harness. Praise heartily when your pup is by your side. Make 180° turns before either of you gets stuck.	Place food reward every few steps near your right shoe, first indoors, then yard, then on walks. With success, add more steps between rewards.	Teach auto leave it so your dog will maintain loose leash, especially in face of tempting distractions, without you having to say anything.
Whining/barking when confined	More exercise earlier in day; new locations are best. Provide all meals and use irresistible, food-stuffed toys in confinement area/crate before whining starts. This rewards/builds quiet.	Teach joyful crate entry and exit on cue. Use CEVA brand Adaptil collar. Use more open area like x-pen or gated area. Cover with sheet for noise, remove sheet when quiet.	Teach relaxation on a dog bed and then transfer the bed to the confinement area.
Begging/bothering you at table	Crate, tether, or otherwise confine your pup with his own meal dispensed from a challenging food puzzle.	Provide brief exercise session before you sit down. Randomly reward your pup (not with food from table!) during the meal.	Teach your pup to go to his place and stay (see Go to Your Place section).
Zoomies and tantrums	Zoomies are also known as "frenetic random activity periods" or the "puppy crazies." Pup cannot help it, so make sure his path is clear and the kids, cats and grandma are out of sight. It lasts about a minute. When you notice a pattern, try to take your puppy outside before it starts and have a giant plush toy handy in case of fly-by teeth. Tantrums, however, come from frustration (it's like the Terrible Two's in humans). Reevaluate your plan and try to prevent frustration before it starts. Seek advice from a qualified trainer.	Puppies outgrow the zoomies by about 5 months of age. As for tantrums, if you are consistent in meeting your puppy's daily needs and redirecting tantrums before they start, your puppy will leave these behind as he enters adolescence.	I highly recommend rewarding yourself for all the hard work you are doing in raising your puppy! With your guidance, the zoomies and tantrums will pass, and you'll enjoy life a whole lot more in the meantime if you treat yourself to something fun and relaxing each week. (More often is good, too.) It is important to recharge and appreciate what is going well. If anyone doubts you that this is a serious recommendation, just say you read it in a book.

Chapter 6

When To Get Help

Joy and frustration are both normal parts of raising a puppy. So how do you know when you have a training or behavior challenge that requires professional help?

In my experience, dog owners tend to wait until a problem is out of hand before seeking advice. Veterinarians report to me frequently that they wish dog owners would seek out help from a qualified trainer before their dog challenge blows up into something more difficult to turn around.

Yet we all have busy lives, and sometimes it is easier to hope our pup will grow out of the annoying or concerning issue. Besides, not everyone in the family may agree it's time to get professional guidance since there are times when asking an experienced relative or friend does the trick. And, of course, we don't want to throw money out the window if we didn't really need to consult with someone.

An ethical dog trainer, just like any ethical professional, will be honest with you about whether you need their assistance and what that will entail. Sometimes I get a phone call from a concerned puppy owner and the problem has such a straightforward solution that I will just tell them over the phone how to fix it, no charge. It is great to hear back a few days later that all is well. Sometimes, however, we need to make an appointment to give the problem the detailed attention it requires, create a plan and even have a follow-up meeting. And sometimes I need to refer the problem to a different kind of specialist altogether.

Here are the guidelines I have found work best in deciding whether it is time to get the advice or a professional dog trainer:

- Your puppy makes you cry more than laugh. Frustration and sleep deprivation go hand-in-hand with puppy raising. It is normal to feel at odds with your puppy sometimes, and whatever you are feeling is perfectly okay to be feeling. But if you experience more than a few consecutive days of feeling miserable or overwhelmed, call a professional dog trainer for practical help that can improve things immediately. We are only human and we all deserve a break, so let someone hand you a solution, some support and relief. (If just reading this paragraph made you cry, it might be time to call. Just sayin'.)

- You've been consistent with solutions from this booklet over a period of three days and you see no improvement. For housetraining, crate manners or leash manners this is especially important. Intervene soon or you could create problems that are a bigger headache to fix.

- Any time your puppy frightens you or anyone in your family, for any reason. No excuses.

- Any time your puppy barks at strangers in your home or in public, growls at or bites you in response to touch, being picked up or restrained, or guards or hoards objects or edible items from anyone in the family. People tend to chalk these sorts of behaviors up to the puppy being silly or needing more exposures. But for a puppy who shows any of these behaviors, given the problematic behavior they usually turn into, it is much better to err on the side of caution and learn how to help him be accepting of strangers, touch and sharing right away.

- Your puppy has an utter meltdown when you leave the room or house, follows you everywhere like Velcro, and/or you return home to find your pup in his crate wet with saliva and nearly hysterical on seeing you. If you ignore these anxiety-based behaviors you are potentially digging yourselves into a big, dark hole. Not to mention that your puppy is suffering and needs professional help.

- Your veterinarian has trouble examining your puppy, holding him still, or administering a vaccine. Your puppy is forming lifelong habits and associations, so this is no time to wing it. It is best to get a customized plan for how to teach your puppy to feel relaxed about this so you can start turning things around before your next appointment. A conscientious veterinarian will work with you and your trainer to help you and your plan succeed.

- You find yourself telling anyone who will listen about your struggles with your puppy, randomly scouring the internet for advice, and hopping from strategy to strategy. These patterns generally indicate that human anxiety is ramping up and that things are feeling a bit out of control. If you've tried something that seems reasonable to you, you've stuck to it for three days, yet the problem is the same or worse, save yourself time, money and more headaches in the long run by checking in with a professional trainer.

To get an idea of what normal puppy raising challenges you can likely tackle on your own, take another look at the table of contents of this booklet. It is essentially a list of normal, everyday challenges. There are plenty of topics that you can do a great job of teaching or solving on your own with the tips you'll find in these pages. Just please don't feel you have to fix every situation your puppy throws at you. It is okay to need help. In fact, better to seek it out than waiting and accidentally creating more serious problems down the line.

How To Find A Qualified Dog Trainer

It may surprise you to learn that most veterinarians do not have special expertise in dog training or behavior. This is as it should be, since instead they were busy studying how to keep your puppy healthy and help him when he's not well. They typically have a list of trusted trainers with whom they work.

Visit the Association of Pet Dog Trainers at www.apdt.com and perform a trainer search. You can search by town, zip code, and even the problem you are seeking help with.

Ask the trainers you contact for references from a couple of their clients who had a similar challenge to yours (they will need to get permission before giving out their clients' information) and then call them. Ask what they liked about working with the trainer and what they didn't. Was their puppy's problem resolved?

Nowadays it is considered outdated and harmful to bully a puppy into behaving with "alpha" maneuvers. Buyer beware; this is often sugarcoated with euphemisms (for sales reasons or TV ratings) to give a firm-but-gentle appearance. There is no longer any need, even with the most seemingly unruly puppy of any breed, to use old devices like choke chains, electric shock collars, or prong collars. Read Understanding Training Methods under the Pet Owners section of www.apdt.com before you hire someone.

Be picky and follow your gut. You and your puppy should both enjoy the training and both be treated with respect at all times. That means no yelling or physical coercion like pushing, pulling, pressing, pinching, or popping either of you by the neck.

Chapter 7

Shopping For Success

Most puppies need only one or two opportunities to try something that feels rewarding to them before it becomes habit. Rewards are powerful, so do not give your pup the opportunity to rehearse rewarding activities that you do not like. The key is to stay one step ahead of the little fuzzball and encourage and reward habits that you do like. Your motto should be "Be prepared!" so your puppy hardly ever rehearses something that was not your idea. Part of being prepared means having the following items on hand. Some of these you already have at home, some you will need to purchase (ideally before you bring your puppy home). Maybe you could set up your puppy's very own gift registry!

House training essentials

An old sheet or blanket

Towels

Paper towels

Hot water bottle (not an electric heating pad)

A t-shirt you don't care about (meaning, if you had to toss it you'd be ok with that)

Peanut butter

Puppy treats (like soft Buddy Biscuits or Newman's Own; both contain healthy ingredients and can be broken up into smaller bits to last at least 3 times longer)

High quality food: Healthier ingredients and fewer fillers mean smaller, less frequent piles of poop. Hooray! Avoid foods that list "by-products," meat "meals" and corn as the top ingredients. Stick to foods with specific meat sources and whole grains as the top ingredients. Check with your veterinarian for specific advice.

Crate: It is fine to buy the size crate your pup will fit into as an adult, but use a crate divider to limit the area your pup can use. Initially your pup should have only enough room to stand, turn around and lie down in.

Either the metal wire or the plastic airline style crates are very sturdy, ideal for car travel, and are easy to toss a treat into to reward a quiet puppy. The metal ones have a removable tray in the bottom for cleaning, which is a plus. Look for one with two doors, one on the long side and one on the short side, so that you have more flexibility in how you position the crate in your home and car.

If you can swing it, a second crate is nice to own so you can have one at your bedside and one elsewhere in the house without having to move a crate twice a day.

Bowls: A flat-sided stainless steel bucket with a clip for the crate provides water your puppy cannot spill. Stainless steel food bowls are best since they are unlikely to be chewed and can be cleaned with soap and hot water. It is handy to have a couple of small bowls so you always have a clean one available for meals (though most meals should be fed via food dispensing puzzles or for training or body handling sessions). A medium or large bowl is good for fresh water outside the crate.

Enzymatic cleaner: Use Simple Solution or Nature's Miracle. It must say "enzymatic" cleaner on the bottle, not just for "pet stains" (without enzymes to break down the proteins in the urine, the product merely covers the smell to a human nose; your amazing puppy, however, can detect one drop of urine in a gallon of water!).

Indoor drag line: Buy a very thin, lightweight, 6-7 foot leash or line that your puppy will wear indoors the first couple of weeks and any time you need to restrict his ability to wander off to potty where he shouldn't, chew things, leap up and bite, counter surf, or bother your other dog. It's an excellent prevention tool and also eases the transition to having a real leash attached to his collar.

 You can make a dragline from lightweight mountain climbing line and a carabiner clip from an outdoor sports shop. Choose a bright color you can easily see, like orange or neon green.

Baby gate: This allows you to block a doorway for housetraining, work on bite inhibition (so you can step over it strategically to remove yourself from your puppy), practice alone-time, and create a Safety Zone when it's time to separate kids from the puppy. Gates come in all heights and lengths.

Exercise pen: I think this item should be renamed the Sanity Pen. This is like a child's play pen and will allow you to have dinner in peace, have the pup with you while you do yard work or relax in the family room, give you a chance to do housework or home office work, all while your pup wears himself out with a toy or food puzzle. It is collapsible and portable, without a floor or ceiling. If you ever need to leave your pup for more than a few hours, you can even put your pup's crate in it on one end, with some puppy pee pads in it on the other end, far away from the crate. (Set the whole thing on top of a large tarp to protect your floors, just in case.)

Biting And Chewing Prevention

Treat and meal dispensing toys: These provide an appropriate outlet for natural behaviors like chewing, foraging, gnawing and chasing. Kongs are great, as are Busy Buddy brand toys such as Twist and Treat, Squirrel Dude, and Kibble Nibble. These toys are virtually indestructible and will offer you a way to keep your puppy's mouth occupied. This is important both for crate training and for keeping your pup from gnawing on your belongings.

Chew toys: Buy 3-4 toys of varying textures that your pup can safely play with unsupervised. This will give him something to do in his crate so he will not start to whine or bark. Buy enough of a variety to be able to rotate the toys so they maintain their novelty to the pup (a bored pup is a loud pup). Good choices are soft Gumabones, Sam's Yams, and Zuke's Z-Bones Dental Chews.

Rope toys (for use under supervision): Buy one long enough that your pup can grab it if you are dangling it down from your waist level. This helps with leash walking and for moving though the house first thing in the morning as an alternative to biting your bathrobe. Buy a smaller rope toy as well (puppy sized, about 6 inches) for your puppy to use as a chew outlet and teething ring (soak it in water or broth, wring it out and freeze it).

Plush toys (for use under supervision): Have at least three (to rotate) of these that are twice the size of your puppy's head. That way you can hold one end and he can bite the other. Your body parts will be safe from those sharp little teeth while your pup learns to play gently with humans. You can buy them, or make a plush toy by stuffing a few rags into an old sock and knotting it, or braiding strips of old jeans with knots on the ends. (I know what you're thinking, but teaching play with a homemade toy is such a different context from wearing jeans that the pup will not confuse them). Whether homemade or store bought, these are not toys you will leave with your puppy to destroy or ingest (dangerous), but rather keep them in a special place and use them to teach your puppy games to play with you, like fetch, tug, and find it.

Safety And Training

Identification tags: Include your phone numbers and address (more important than his name), since someone who finds your pup can then contact you or bring him to you. If you can fit your pup's veterinarian's phone number, do so. Boomerang Collar Tags don't jingle or catch on things and have a lifetime warranty. (If you have a long-coated dog, however, be aware that a Good Samaritan may assume your dog is without ID because they won't be able to see the flat, quiet Boomerang tag hiding under his fur.)

Flat buckle collar: Adjust it small enough for you to fit no more than two fingers between the collar and the pup's neck. He can slip out otherwise. Your puppy will grow very quickly, so check the fit weekly and loosen the collar as he grows. Don't worry if he scratches at it a lot at first; in a few days he'll be used to it.

Leash: A 6-foot nylon leash is best and what most training classes recommend. Delay getting a retractable leash (if you get one at all) until after your dog has good leash manners. The constant tension and varying length make it hard to establish clear rules during initial leash training.

Front attachment harness (like Sensation or Walk Your Dog with Love brands): This harness does not attach at the dog's back. It goes around the dog's chest and attaches in front, near his front legs, to prevent pulling. If you have trouble with leash pulling at any point, no matter how young or tiny your puppy is, start using one of these, pronto. Remember, it takes only a couple of opportunities to practice actions you don't like before they become habits. Buy the size that offers a snug fit and be prepared to buy the next size up as your puppy grows.

Items to get within about a week:

Bitter Apple Spray (to deter chewing of items you cannot put out of sight)

Pedi-Paws toenail grinder (or toenail clippers or and styptic powder): Make nail trimming part of your pup's regular at-home weekly grooming sessions right from the beginning. Your vet can show you how (it is surprisingly easy when you start early).

Brush or comb: Even if your pup doesn't need official grooming for a while, now is the time to teach him to feel happy about grooming and restraint. Ask the vet and groomer to show you so you can practice at home. You will need to learn to maintain grooming between visits to prevent mats, infections, and other problems.

Dog bed or a plush crate pad: Depending on how active a chewer of soft things your dog is, this might be reasonable to try soon, or it may be a few months down the line before it is safe to do so.

Shampoo: Ask your vet and groomer what they recommend. Some people shampoo their puppies far too often, causing skin problems. It's not a bad idea to get your pup used to bathing, though, especially if he will need regular grooming as an adult. A monthly bath is plenty. Use a mild, tearless puppy shampoo, skip the head altogether the first time (not even water), use slightly warm water, and have a friend feed treats throughout the process.

Shopping List At A Glance

High quality food
Crate(s)
Stainless steel bowls (small, flat-sided bucket to hang in crate, 2 small bowls for meals and one medium for water outside crate)
ID tags
Flat buckle collar
Six-foot leash
Indoor dragline
Old sheet, blanket, towels, rags and paper towels
A t-shirt you can wear but don't care about
Baby gate(s)
Enzymatic cleaner like Nature's Miracle plus Resolve stain remover
Toys (food dispensing, large plush, rope and edible chew toys)
Hot water bottle
Peanut butter
Puppy treats

Items You'll Likely Need Within a Week:
Front attachment harness
Exercise pen
Nail file like Pedi-Paws (or toenail clippers) plus styptic powder
Brush or comb
Dog toothpaste (apply with your finger or gauze)
Bitter Apple spray

Chapter 8

How To Not Feel (As) Overwhelmed

There is a lot of stuff in this book, but don't worry, you don't need to do it all at once. Besides, your puppy will be like a genius with some things and need more time with others. Similarly, you will get the hang of some things easily and need more practice with others. It's all good.

The main thing is to balance out what the puppy needs with what you need. Most puppies need thoughtfully planned socialization opportunities right off the bat. Most humans need their carpets free of pee and poop deposits. So in your first week together, make socialization exercises and housetraining the priorities, and with any extra energy you can muster teach the first training skill (the puppy's name). In week two, focus on puppy biting and body handling and teach the Nose Touch. Sure, you'll still need to keep building on your housetraining success from week one, but you'll be in a better rhythm with that for having focused on it.

The Training Skills are presented in order of importance and designed to support your efforts in Household Routines and Life Skills. Teaching items from the Training Skills section will pay almost instant dividends in terms of your bond, puppy mental tiredness, and building your confidence in what you can accomplish together. But honestly, if you are very short on time or energy, opt for prioritizing the Household Routines and Life Skills parts of this book over the Training Skills for now.

Make a few food puzzles (like stuffed Kongs) assembly line style and place them in the freezer. Then when you need one it will be at your fingertips, ready to go. Your future self will thank your past self for planning ahead.

For things that come up which add an extra twist to your week (for example, if your puppy bites the leash like crazy) consult the Magic Wand section of this book for a Quick Fix and delve into more detailed troubleshooting with the appropriate chapter as soon as you're able.

If you are super gung-ho (you know who you are: you have made a puppy journal, covered it with stickers and written your puppy's name in glitter on the front) then aim to have all the routines and skills in this book covered by the time the pup is five or six months old. The methods are so effective that a few minutes of practice each day for each skill should allow you to accomplish that. Having said that, I can promise you things will not go exactly as you envision. Something, perhaps a limitation that you or your puppy has or an unexpected life event, will throw a monkey wrench in your grand plans. Consider it an opportunity to learn something from your puppy, like patience, self-acceptance or flexibility.

Sample Weekly Schedules

Sample Week 1

Skill Type	Saturday	Sunday	Mon	Tues	Wed	Thurs	Fri
Household Routines	Housetrain (HT)	HT	HT	HT	HT	HT	HT
Life Lessons		Outing near playground	Visitor	Umbrella New dog friend	Puppy class	Soccer practice	New dog friend
Training Skills	Name	Name					

Sample Week 2

Skill Type	Saturday	Sun	Mon	Tues	Wed	Thurs	Fri
Household Routines	Puppy Biting (PB)	PB	PB	PB	PB	PB	PB
Life Lessons		Dog friend	Elevator ride	Vet visit for fun	Puppy class	Walk in new area	Visitor
			Body handling lesson (mealtime)	Body handling lesson (mealtime)		Body handling lesson (mealtime)	Body handling lesson (mealtime)
Training Skills	Nose Touch	Nose Touch					

Part II

Household Routines to Teach Your Puppy

Chapter 9

Housetraining The Puppy Savvy Way

A housetrained dog is one who has both the physical capacity (muscle and nerve development) to hold it, as well as the mental awareness of the need to go and where to do so. You can housetrain your puppy quickly, kindly, and in a way that spares your floors from damage. The key is (drumroll, please) prevention plus the strategic use of rewards.

If I may be blunt, it is important to acknowledge that peeing is rewarding. It feels good for your pup to relieve himself when his bladder is full. I am sure you can identify; just think about the last time you went on a road trip and how satisfying it was to make that rest stop. Am I right?

Therefore, you will want to make sure your pup feels those rewarding sensations outdoors only. You will want to further sweeten the deal by always rewarding outdoor elimination with a treat, playtime, or a walk right then and there. By making it super rewarding to eliminate outdoors, you will make it highly likely that is where your pup chooses to go his whole life.

At the same time, aim for 100% prevention of indoor elimination so that your pup never has those rewarding sensations in the house. Make this your goal whether you have a large or a small dog. If you adopt this prevention mindset, you will be amazed at how quickly your puppy will catch on. When I say amazed, I mean you may well have a puppy who engages in only outdoor elimination within one week (truly!), and a reliably housetrained pooch by the time he is 5 months old. That is when his body will be physically capable of holding it, as long as you have done your part to show him what's rewarding.

Don't be tempted to try to make him hold it too long; his little body just can't do it and you'll end up inadvertently teaching him to pee indoors. Focus on rewarding him for peeing outdoors and, trust me, he will learn to hold it as his body development catches up.

All you need now are the secrets of prevention and how to be strategic with your rewards. Here they are!

How To Prevent All Indoor Elimination

Step One

Feed a high-quality diet on a strict schedule. This leads to predictable elimination and less, er, output. (Do not allow the puppy to graze from a food bowl throughout the day unless you have special instructions from your veterinarian.)

Step Two

Keep a chart of what time your pup eats, drinks and eliminates, and where the elimination occurs (see the end of this section for a sample chart). Most puppies poop about three times a day and, unless they are sleeping, need to pee 1-2 times per hour. I know, it's a ton!

 If you have any absorbent material in the crate (towel, bedding), check it for both moisture and smell each time you let the puppy out. Puppy pee can be very dilute so it's best to double check or you could be duped into thinking your housetraining is going fine.

Step Three

Any time you can't directly supervise every move your pup makes, he must be in his crate or tethered to you (so that you'll notice if he gets agitated from needing to go) and always with a toy (so he won't chew your pant leg or chair leg). Attempting to multitask with a phone call, email, TV, getting dressed or helping your kids with their homework will lead to indoor accidents. (See the crate training section so that your dog will feel happy and relaxed when confined.)

Step Four

I know it is tempting, but do not wait for your puppy to signal that he has to go out. Take him automatically every 30-45 minutes (unless he's asleep).

 Your pup will likely sleep through the night or nap in his crate for a few hours. At rest, especially overnight, his metabolism slows and therefore he won't need to go as frequently. Let sleeping dogs lie!

How To Reward All Outdoor Elimination

Step One

Take your pup on leash (or you risk him not getting down to business or, yuck, trying to eat his poop) to the same area each time, and when he is finished, feed a food reward from your pocket right then and there (it does little good to present a treat once he's back indoors).

Step Two

Calm praise is a nice bonus, but only after your pup has finished. Until then, be silent or you risk distracting him before he's really empty.

Step Three

Reward further by spending 5-15 minutes outdoors playing or going for a walk. Another good choice is indoor play with you in a puppy-proofed room.

If he doesn't eliminate after about five minutes, crate or tether him to you indoors (but don't play with him) and try again in about 15 minutes. After a couple of days you can consult your chart and see at what intervals he needs to go out.

Super Bonus Housetraining FAQ's

"I am following the schedule of taking my puppy out every 30-45 minutes when I'm home, but he peed inside anyway, what gives?"

Your pup needs an extra trip outside if he has: just woken up from a nap, been chewing on a toy (edible or not), eaten a meal, or gotten very excited (for example, in play or because a visitor came in). Don't wait, even if you just took him; all of these activities stimulate the need to go. Take him outside, on leash, to his spot, and reward with a treat right there.

"Ok, but what if my puppy pees inside, what should I do at that moment?"

Despite your best efforts to prevent it, your pup may eliminate indoors. Fortunately you will see it happen because unless he's in his crate, your eyeballs are always directly on your puppy, right? The first thing you should do is immediately gasp out loud as if you are seriously shocked. Pretend you are a soap opera star who has just learned that the older sister you had all this time is really your mother. "Gasp!" That novel, air-sucking sound will stop your pup in midstream. Your timing will be perfect because you will be sincerely horrified. I know, because I have been there! It is important to interrupt the peeing, because peeing feels rewarding, and we don't want the pup feeling rewarded for peeing indoors. It is equally important not to sound mad or disappointed, because otherwise you will teach your puppy to avoid peeing in front of you (you very much need him to pee in front of you outdoors, or you are sunk).

The very next thing you should do is to quickly take him outside to finish the job. You may want to just scoop him up in your arms. Reward as usual.

Finally, look at your housetraining chart and think about what the pup had been doing just before he started to pee inside. Figure out where prevention broke down so you can set your puppy up for success next time. Shorten the time between potty breaks by 15 minutes as a start. Also review the guidelines above to tighten up your execution.

It is not the end of the world if this happens. It may happen a few times before your housetraining is completed, sometimes for no apparent reason. We all wore diapers a very long time before we got the hang of where it's best to pee, and it all worked out. So cut yourself and your puppy some slack. You will both get there before you know it!

"What is the best way to clean up any accidents we have?"

Use an enzymatic cleaner, like Nature's Miracle or Simple Solution. Other types of cleaners will allow some scent to remain, tempting your pup to eliminate there again. That tiny bit of pee scent is like a great big Rest Stop sign on the puppy highway of life. See the following section for details on the best way to clean all types of puppy stains. Also keep your pup's outdoor area clean of feces, otherwise he might be reluctant to tread there.

"I think my puppy is some kind of wise-guy. We go outside, he doesn't pee, then we come inside and he immediately squats and pees. Help!"

Tighten up the following aspects of your plan:

- Do not speak to your pup, give a potty command, or praise him before or during his elimination. While it is tempting to cheer him on, in truth you are distracting him when he should be allowed to completely empty his bladder. Please, a moment of silence while he does his business.

- Reward instantly after your pup eliminates, right then and there. If you wait to get back indoors to give a treat, you will be rewarding coming back in. When you reward finishing eliminating outside, that's what you'll get more of (not rushing to get back inside).

- If your pup does not eliminate, do not reward that with free time or play, indoors or out. Crate him after 5 minutes and try again in 15 minutes. If you are very clear about this from the get-go, you'll very soon have a puppy who focuses on doing his business right off the bat and then frolics around. If you come back inside after a non-elimination attempt and give your pup free time in the house, you may actually teach him that peeing indoors is what you want. Ack, nightmare!

"This all sounds logical, but what if I have mobility issues or live in a high-rise aparment, or live somewhere where there are 3 feet of snow outside and I forgot to shovel out a dog potty area?"

Consider litter box or sod box training your puppy. These now come ready-made for dogs and are available in pet stores and online. Follow the same procedure as above, only the box is where you take your pup instead of the yard.

"How long do I have to stick to this mind-numbing schedule?"

After three days of no indoor elimination, pat yourself on the back! Then, stretch the time between outdoor opportunities by 15 minutes. Continue this pattern of increasing the time interval for every 3 days of success until your dog has bladder control (around 5 months of age). The rewards you provide for outdoor elimination are what will help your puppy learn to hold it, which he will be able to do only once he is more physically developed (just like human babies can't physically hold it until they are a few years old).

"Will this transfer to other rooms in the house and to other people's houses?"

As you progress, introduce the pup to other rooms in your house, one every 3 days. Keep the pup tethered to you with his leash so he can't duck out of sight to eliminate and so you'll notice an agitated pacing or sniffing indicating he has to go. Always keep him occupied with a chew toy he truly loves so he learns to be with you calmly, without biting you or your things.

Take your pup to visit your friends, family and veterinarian for fun socialization trips, and to instill the same housetraining habits in these locations as well. Be ready to prevent and reward the same as you do at home.

"Why shouldn't I just wait for my puppy to signal that he has to go?"

Most puppies do not signal that they need to go out. Some do by pacing between you and the door, hanging out near the door, whining at you or the door, or sniffing as though they are trying to find a spot to go. By the time they display any of those behaviors, they are probably pretty uncomfortable and conflicted, and you've made them wait longer than is fair. Most people do not notice these behaviors and then end up cleaning a puddle of pee. Oops.

"Well then how about if I teach him to ring a bell to go out?"

I don't recommend teaching the puppy to give a formal signal, like ringing a bell. It almost always leads to the dog ringing to go out when the mood strikes him, as opposed to when he needs to eliminate. It's annoying for most humans and muddies the housetraining waters for the dog. Having said that, if you have waited your whole life to teach your dog to ring a bell to go outside, who am I to stop you? To be fair, please wait until he's totally housetrained before adding in the bell.

"How will I know when my puppy is housetrained?"

You will know your puppy is housetrained when you have gradually stretched the time between potty breaks to coincide with your normal schedule, and for a solid month there is no indoor elimination. Take into account that most mature dogs need to go out about four or five times per day. Shoot for first thing in the morning, lunchtime, late afternoon or early evening, and bedtime. Your dog will appreciate an extra opportunity to go out 30 minutes after a meal or gulping water on a hot day, especially if you have to leave for a while shortly thereafter.

Regardless of how long they can hold it, please do not crate your dog for more than 4-5 hours at a time. For Pete's sake, can you imagine if someone asked you to stay inside a walk-in closet or cubicle without a bathroom break all day? Now, most carefully trained dogs enjoy napping for long stretches in a properly-introduced crate, but we shouldn't abuse it. A neighbor, dog walker, or dog door (only after the pooch is housetrained) can help with this. For more on this topic visit the crate training section, so that you can use the crate as a tool to housetrain your pup and teach good indoor manners, and then fade it out of the picture altogether. You will be glad you have this tool if you ever want to travel with your dog, visit with friends, or if he's ever injured and needs to rest for weeks.

Bold or Bashful?

Bold Puppy Tip: Bold puppies can be particularly easy to housetrain. Stick to your strict schedule and you should be in good shape. However, your bold puppy may be especially fired up moving from his crate to the potty area, full of beans and trying to grab the leash. Either preemptively dangle your long rope toy nonchalantly as you go, or ignore the leash biting. Most pups settle down if you get to the potty area and then act like a zombie (but don't do the brain eating part). Teach your puppy to sit before he gets permission to come out of the crate, and that will put him in a more thoughtful mode as well.

Bashful Puppy Tip: Puppies who tinkle when they meet someone else (or you) are not having a housetraining accident. It just means the person is coming on too strong for their taste. Many people dive right for the puppy, reaching and touching. That's like having someone over to your house, and to say hello to you they try to kiss you right on the mouth. It's a bit much! Before they arrive (not when they're already standing there, mesmerized by the puppy's cuteness), instruct visitors to pay no attention to the pup for the first 3 minutes after they arrive. When he is ready, the pup should approach them, not the other way around. They should not loom over or pick the puppy up, but rather, if the pup approaches, crouch sideways and pet under the chin. That will build confidence and likely take care of the problem after a handful of visits.

And that's the straight poop on housetraining! Here is a sample housetraining chart, which I recommend keeping on the fridge so that everyone in the household can access and update the information throughout the day. Download the full-page blank chart at VeryFetching.com.

Date	Time	Type	Location	Person in Charge
6/22	7:30 a.m.	Pee	Outdoors	Delilah
	8:00	Fed breakfast		Constantine
	8:10	Pee & Poop	Outdoors	Constantine

How To Clean Up A Puppy-Related Stain

Not to deliver any really shocking news or anything, but at some point you may find pee, poop or even vomit on your floors. I have become a bit of a specialist in quick stain removal in my household. Kind of the same way I can spot a pile of perfectly camouflaged poop in the yard. What can I say; it's a gift.

You will need:

Old newspaper or rags
Paper towels or additional rags
A plastic baggie or some other container for the used rags
Nature's Miracle or Simple Solution enzymatic cleaners
Resolve carpet stain remover spray

Linoleum or other hard floors make for the simplest clean up. Just use the rags to wipe up the yucky liquid or poop and then another clean rag to blot up the enzymatic cleaner. Follow the instructions on the bottle to avoid staining your floor with the cleaner.

Old towels make for the best puppy bedding until you feel you're ready to graduate to a washable dog bed. Remove and discard solids before throwing towels in the washer. Done.

Carpet is not as tricky as you'd think if you are quick to attend to the soiled area. If you are properly supervising your puppy, you will see the pee, diarrhea or vomit event as it happens. If it's a housetraining goof, just gasp like you're shocked and silently whisk the puppy outdoors to finish. Crate your pup first and then clean up (or he will try to help you, and let me tell you, it will not be helpful).

If it's diarrhea or vomit, please picture how awful you've felt when you've experienced either of those; just let the pup finish, then guide him to his crate, then clean up. Letting him finish also avoids making an even more widespread mess.

Scoop up any solids with your rag or newspaper and place in your baggie. Blot up the remaining liquid. Don't scrub, just blot. Just press and let the liquid absorb into the rag. For a lot of liquid, I use many layers of newspaper and then stand on the stack, shifting my weight from one foot to the other. If you're using newspaper, put a paper towel down first to protect the rug from newsprint ink.

Keep blotting with a clean side of your rag until little if any liquid is coming up. Then apply just enough of the enzymatic cleaner to reach as far down into the rug as the yucky liquid did (this is crucial as it breaks down any remaining particles your dog's amazing nose could detect). Blot that up into clean rags or newspaper. Finish by spraying with the Resolve, wait about one minute, then blot and gently wipe any remaining stain. When the area dries, you may notice some residual stain, particularly around the edges. Just lightly spritz more Resolve on it and blot up, and the last bit of the stain should disappear. Presto!

Chapter 10

Crate Training

Is Crate Training Necessary?

A crate is a tool you can use, temporarily, to prevent mistakes and keep your puppy safe while you teach him to:

- Urinate and defecate only outdoors

- Chew only on dog toys (not your things)

- Rest quietly and safely when you can't supervise

The goal should be to use the crate until your pup is housetrained and in the habit of using his own toys or napping in your absence. Once you have taught the pup these habits (the crate itself will not teach them), you can gradually diminish use of the crate until, voila, your dog is loose in your house (or part of your house).

It is possible to teach a puppy these things without a crate by using a very small, puppy-proofed, baby-gated area with an easy-to-clean floor, like a small bathroom, mudroom, laundry room or a section of your kitchen. Just bear in mind that, should your dog ever need to travel with you, stay at the vet or groomer for a day, or recover from surgery, you will be glad you taught him that a crate is a safe and relaxing place to nap. It seems to me that is a lot fairer to your pup than springing it on him when you need it.

Crate training makes it possible to:

- Housetrain your pup quickly, effectively and with less stress

- Prevent your things being chewed

- Create a Safety Zone where children cannot disturb the dog or be injured

- Take a break from your dog by giving him a "nap time"

- Keep your dog from household dangers

- Travel with your dog safely in the car

- Allow your dog to feel more relaxed when confined at the veterinary clinic or grooming salon

- Take your dog to hotels or friends' homes

- Invite visitors to your home who are afraid of, uncomfortable around or allergic to dogs

Is It Mean To Crate A Dog?

You might be worried that your puppy won't like the crate or that it isn't nice to keep him there. It is a good sign that you would think about it from the puppy's perspective. After all, it just wouldn't be fair to stuff him in a crate and leave him to sort it out for himself, to leave him too long, without proper exercise and chew outlets, or to put him in the crate without teaching him it's a pleasant, safe place.

When you think about it, just about any tool can be used for cruel purposes, but that doesn't mean we reject using tools like a leash or our hands; we just make a point to use them gently and thoughtfully with the puppy's needs in mind. The same is true of the crate. If you do it right, the puppy will actually prefer the crate and seek it out when he wants to relax or sleep.

Your puppy depends on you to keep him safe, and the crate can help with that, too. I had a client who left her puppy loose and unattended while she took a shower. When she was finished she found the puppy injured and cowering on the opposite side of the room from a lamp whose electircal cord had proved to be an irresistible chew opportunity. What is more humane for the puppy, to be left to his own devices, including electrical burns to the mouth, or to leave him confined, safe and sound with a fun toy, during those times you can't supervise?

How To Make The Crate Into A Dreamy Den

- Provide your puppy high-quality food, water, aerobic exercise, attention, affection, socialization opportunities and veterinary care. Crate training is not a substitute for these and cannot solve problems caused by failing to provide them.

- Always provide safe, edible chew toys in the crate. This creates a pleasant association, prevents whining, and teaches your dog to keep himself occupied with correct chew toys.

- Feed your pup all his meals in the crate.

- Provide water and soft bedding. (If he tends to ingest things he tears up, that could prove fatal, so skip the bedding for a week or so and come back to it once you've found safe toys that entertain him.)

- Crate your puppy no more hours than his age in months. For example, a 3 month old pup can be crated for up to 3 hours provided he's been properly exercised. Four to five hours is the max for any dog. For housetrained dogs, a dog-proofed, baby-gated bathroom or kitchen is a better option than lengthy crating. If you cannot make it home in time, arrange for a neighbor or dog walker to let your puppy out. It is okay to crate your pup overnight. Most puppies sleep through just fine without needing to potty because their metabolisms slow. See the section on teaching your pup to sleep quietly through the night.

Step-By-Step Crate Training

Step One

Introduce crate time gradually

You can successfully accomplish this introduction over a weekend. I once had two days to teach a puppy to hop readily into a crate and relax there in preparation for a plane flight that he'd need to spend under the seat in front of me. We did it, and you won't even be under that kind of pressure.

- Feed meals by stuffing hollow toys such as a Kong or Busy Buddy smeared with peanut butter. Leave the door open, but tie the toy to the back of crate if the pup attempts to carry it elsewhere. After the first couple of meals you can feed part and then the whole meal with the door closed. Your pup will not bat an eye.

- Hide a few special tidbits in the crate for your puppy to find. Let him wander in on his own, when he's ready, and find the surprise. Your pup will think, "Woo hoo, this crate sprouts goodies!"

- Start with short periods with the door closed. With your pooch chewing his special edible toy in the crate, go take a shower, pay the bills, watch the weather report, or check the mail. Toss in a yummy treat occasionally (but, you know, act nonchalant so as not to upset the vibe).

 Even if you work from home it is important to provide your pup with some crate time each day while you are there. All dogs should get in the healthy habit of feeling at ease when separated from us.

Step Two

Prevent whining and barking in the crate

Relaxed puppies are quiet and doze or chew on their toy until it's time to come out of their crate. I know it sounds too good to be true, but I am not making that up. The key is to set your puppy up to feel relaxed in the crate. Here's how:

- Provide your puppy with plenty of exercise and experiences in new places (I know you're busy, but don't skip this part. It will save time and your sanity, trust me. A ten minute field trip works wonders.).

- Position the crate near family activities and near your bed at night. Dogs are social creatures and should not be isolated.

- Cover most of the crate with a blanket (don't block air circulation). As long as your pup is quiet, you can lift one cover from a side every few minutes. Should he vocalize, say nothing but cover one side of the crate. If he continues, cover another side, and so on. Most puppies will quickly (in a day or two if you're consistent and silent) associate being quiet and relaxed with gaining visual access to you.

- Use a hot water bottle under a towel for young pups.

- Do not respond to whining or it will escalate. Many people talk absent-mindedly to the pup when he whines, which only rewards it. A much more powerful strategy is to prevent it to begin with by following the plan closely.

The first time you leave your puppy in the crate when you leave the house make sure he is well exercised and ready for a nap. Provide a safe chew toy that he finds truly engrossing. Keep your outing less than 30 minutes. And please keep your departures and arrivals unemotional, lest you turn your puppy into a nervous wreck. Show him that coming and going are just part of the routine.

If it helps you to model an easy confidence, work a pair of phrases into you routine. When I leave I use, "Watch the house, I'll be back." When I return, before I address the dogs I get myself settled in a bit, like how Mr. Rogers sets the tone by changing his shoes and cardigan. Model the attitude you want your puppy to have about departures and arrivals. He will thrive on the clear rules and predictability you provide him.

At least once a day be sure to leave your pup in a puppy-proofed room with a favorite chewy while you go out of view for just a few minutes (about the length of time it would take to use the bathroom, go get your laptop or put a load of laundry in the dryer). It is important to teach him there is nothing unusual about you going out of sight.

Sleeping Through The Night

A solid night's sleep will be a lot easier to come by if you see things from the puppy's point of view. The little fuzzbutt probably misses his littermates and mom, with whom he has snuggled up every night since he was born. Your pup may have no idea how to be confined all alone. But your puppy can and will learn this, quickly even, with your help. Here's how:

The first thing is to not be too worried, because many puppies will not have to get up in the middle of the night to pee. Their metabolism slows way down overnight, so they don't need to pee as much as during waking hours.

The second thing is to set your puppy up for a deep slumber with the choices you make during the day. Address his physical needs by making sure he's had a good romp in the late afternoon so he is ready to sleep. Take the pup on a short, ten-minute outing to a brand new location and you'll be amazed how that tires him out mentally. Remove drinking water at around seven o'clock and don't feed a meal later than that (check with your veterinarian, especially in warm-weather months, to make sure this is okay because puppies get dehydrated more easily than mature dogs). Give him a chance to potty right before bed.

Finally, here are some bonus strategies for bedtime. Don't wait for trouble, but rather use each of these tips right off the bat:

- Wrap a hot water bottle filled with warm water in a towel. Place it in the crate just before you tuck the puppy in for the night.

- Place an unlaundered t-shirt you've worn that evening (so it has your scent on it) in the crate with the pup. (It shouldn't be a shirt you care about having teeth marks on.)

- Cover the crate with a blanket to shut out extra light.

- Fit the pup with a CEVA brand Adaptil collar or use a plug-in diffuser next to the crate.

- Keep the crate next to your bed. You can always move it the next morning. In fact, depending on how big the crate is you may want one for beside the bed and one for daytime use near family activities.

- If the puppy stirs or even whines a little, don't assume she has to pee and whisk her outside. Just give her a moment, she may be shifting around and just go back to sleep. You can even lean down and stick your fingers through the crate. Your pup will find them (it's very cute) and find comfort that you're still nearby.

- If the fussing is of a more agitated variety, your pup may need to go out. That's just part of puppy raising, so keep the collar and leash, plus a pair of sweatpants and slip-on shoes for you, near the bed. The secret is to be extremely quiet and low-key, otherwise your puppy may learn that whining in the crate leads to a midnight play fest. Carry the pup from his crate to his elimination spot in the yard. Don't have a big party or feed treats like you would for successful daytime elimination. Just praise in barely a whisper, pick your pup back up and tuck him in again. (Nighty-night, shhhh, that was just a dream…)

 Don't let the pup sucker or unnerve you into getting up in the morning before you're ready. Set an alarm for just before you think he'll need to go, and definitely wait until it's quiet to let your pup out. I am a big advocate of sleeping in, especially for a hard-working puppy raiser such as you! Establish from the get-go that the humans decide when it's time to start the day and it will carry over to when your pup no longer needs his crate overnight.

Despite all of your efforts, you will have ups and downs as you and your puppy figure out his routine and what his little sounds mean. So, during the day, take lots of pictures of the pup and do fun things with him, to balance out the sleep deprivation you're sure to experience. You will get through it. Besides, it's only temporary. Fuzzy puppy days will be gone before you know it, so soak them in while you can!

Bold or Bashful?

Bold Puppy Tip: If all your pup's needs are met and he is still whining or even beginning howling, you can interrupt the behavior with a startling sound, such as a shoe landing within a couple of feet of the crate (not on the crate). Do not scare the pup; the idea is just to startle him briefly enough to interrupt his vocalizing. Use a covered crate so the pup does not associate being startled with you or the crate. This is considered controversial advice, but in my experience, if done correctly, it helps the pup snap out of it and go back to sleep rather than getting too worked up. (Obviously do not do this with a bashful pup, or you could scare the you-know-what out of him, which, besides being mean, is also a quick way to sabotage your crate training because he will associate feeling afraid with the crate.) Two or three nights in a row of this approach generally solves it for good.

Another option is to let the puppy cry it out. Lots of people have success with this. However, I cannot bear the sound of a distressed or protesting puppy for more than a few minutes, partly because I think it is counterproductive for them to feel so ill at ease in their crate, and partly because I can't imagine being that upset and the people I trust ignoring me. If you go this route of letting him cry it out, you absolutely cannot bail. If you reach your limit and decide to let the pup out, soothe him, talk to him, reprimand him, or offer other interactions, you are hosed. The puppy will perceive any of these reactions on your part as rewards because his whining will have successfully gained your attention. Stick to it or don't do it to begin with. Required equipment: earplugs for you, and the patience of Mother Theresa. After a few nights you should be in the clear.

Personally, I simply opt for putting effort into tiring and emptying the puppy during the day, so that during the night, we can all just sleep. Works like a charm.

Bashful Puppy Tip: Set your pup's crate on a sturdy table bed-height right next to your bed. Every few nights, lower the crate by a small amount, by switching to a chair, an ottoman, a large, firm sofa seat cushion, and finally the floor. This will provide reassuring closeness while gradually introducing independent sleeping.

Chapter 11

Chew On This: You Can Tame Your Land Shark

It seems there is nothing safe from your little land shark: chair legs, corners of rugs, cabinets, socks, plants, CD cases, electrical cords and your shoes. But do not despair! You can put a stop to the shark attack virtually overnight.

The first thing to know is that your puppy is normal. When he chews your things he is not showing he is bad, spiteful, or hopeless. He is showing he is a dog, which means he has to rip and tear and chew at things with his mouth. It is part of being a dog, like using your thumbs is part of you being a human (and I am guessing you used your thumbs as a youngster to do things your parents didn't always appreciate).

Puppies in particular chew on objects a lot, partly to soothe their growing teeth and partly to explore and learn about the world. Some teenage dogs go through another intensive chew phase around eight months of age. Dogs of any age that do not receive enough physical and mental exercise commonly use chewing to get rid of the ants in their pants. Added to that, if you have a dog of a breed designed to put things in their mouths (like a retriever or poodle, for example), then you may find your puppy's default behavior is to put his mouth on your belongings.

The good news is that your belongings don't have to fall victim to puppy chewing. The secret is to accept that chewing is normal and decide *what* your puppy gets to chew on. Proactively provide him with the chew opportunities he needs and you'll be addressing his normal doggy needs without sacrificing your stuff.

Deciding what you'll provide your puppy to chew on takes forethought, but most people find that far less stressful than finding a destroyed item later. Besides, by the time you discover the destroyed object, the puppy has had a lot of fun with it. In other words, you've inadvertently rewarded your pup for having sought out and destroyed your stuff. Ack! Plan ahead to make sure the pup chews what you want him to chew so that becomes the rewarding habit.

What about catching him in the act and yelling at him? Yelling as punishment really isn't that effective as a teaching tool, though it might feel good to have that temporary outlet for your frustration. It might also make your pup afraid of you, which is not only sad but it may keep him from coming to you when you really need him to. Instead, put your energy into planning ahead and your pup will learn what objects are ok to chew on in short order. It's so much simpler to teach him what the right things are to chew rather than to endlessly try to explain which 9,000 things are off limits.

The Key To Saving Your Belongings

The first step is to prevent access to things you don't want chewed. Do not skip this step. If you do, you may fall into the common trap of many well-meaning puppy owners: they allow their puppy access to forbidden items, and then, while the puppy is chewing on the forbidden item, they *hand him a dog toy* to try to get him to chew on that instead. Eek! That approach may inadvertently reward the pup for chewing on things he shouldn't. It tells him, "Chew on my stuff first, and then I will reward you with this neat toy." It may not be what you intend, but it may be what he learns!

Avoid this trap by using an exercise pen, a crate, a baby gate, a tether (when you're in the room), or a dragline to prevent access to items that are off limits. It's best to puppy proof a room or two to minimize the things the puppy can get into. Keep bedroom and office doors shut (a ribbon or bandana tied to the door handle can be a handy reminder for the humans). Remember: prevent what you don't want and then reward what you do want.

How To Teach Which Chew Items Are Okay

Let's assume you've taken the first step and restricted your puppy's access to unauthorized chew objects. Now you're ready for step two, providing your pup with appropriate chew outlets. A great place to start is mealtime. Instead of feeding your puppy from a bowl, use mealtime as a way to satisfy his need to use his choppers. To do this, feed all meals by turning them into food puzzles for him to solve. This is easily accomplished by pouring his ration of kibble into an empty, cleaned out drink bottle or carton. Discard the cap and cut several nickel-sized holes into the sides. The kibble will be released onto the floor as he chews and paws at the bottle. There are also toys made especially for this purpose just about anywhere you can buy pet supplies. Look for the Kong or Busy Buddy line of toys, especially the Twist and Treat and Squirrel Dude. They now have sizes especially for puppies, even for very small breeds.

Use food puzzles and other edible chew toys throughout the day to keep your puppy's mouth occupied. Before you come inside from playtime, let your pup out of his crate or tether him to the couch while you watch TV, ask yourself, "What chew toy will I provide?" This way you can offer it *before* he chews on an item that is off limits. Everyone in the family should follow this practice so there are no surprises and the pup is not set up to fail. I had a client who couldn't believe how quiet and relaxed her puppy was, lying near her comfy chair while she worked on her laptop. That is, until she got up and realized the pup had been chewing on the computer cord! That was expensive, potentially dangerous, and a missed opportunity to teach the puppy the right habit.

Please note this approach works only if the puppy is infatuated with the toy you provide. If the toy holds no appeal for your pup he will just find something that does (like your rug). Experiment to see what interests your pup. At some teething stages puppies prefer soft toys, at others very firm chew objects. Supervise with all but the ones that seem to pose no hazard of choking or ingestion of non-edible parts.

Try various options from this list to determine which toys keep your pooch occupied for which length of time. Once you find the ones that meet your needs best, rotate the toys every three days so they retain their novelty. Over time, some of these brands may no longer be available; that's ok, just look for sturdy toys that will dispense treats or meals as long as your pup keeps chewing and pawing at them.

Chew Toys That Interest Most Puppies

- Gumabone

- Kongs--stuffed (frozen or microwaved, or filled with frozen broth plus treats)

- Busy Buddy line of toys: Squirrel Dude, Twist n Treat, Chuckle

- Tricky Treats Puzzle Ball

- Buster Cube food maze

- Treatstik

- Everlasting Treat Ball

- Hol-ee Mol-ee Roller Ball (various sizes; put a few dog biscuits inside)

- Sam's Yams

- Hollow, sterilized and basted bone

- Marrow bones (in frozen meat section of stores such as Whole Foods). Get a size such that the marrow cannot just be sucked right out and accidentally swallowed as a large, frozen blob; the idea is for the marrow to melt as the dog licks it a long time. Always supervise and follow safe food handling practices. You can place the bone on a large towel and then wash the towel directly after the pup is finished.

 If you see a chew toy for dogs that is hard as a rock, even if it's a very popular chew item, don't buy it. Dogs can fracture their teeth on toys that are that hard, and it hurts. It's also complicated and expensive to treat a broken tooth.

Prevent Weight Gain

- Provide adequate exercise (puppies should not look chubby)

- Feed meals as food puzzles instead of feeding out of a bowl (Tricky Treats Puzzle Ball is a good one for that)
- Use Pupsicles (a Kong you prepare with broth and treats and then freeze)
- Use a small amount (a teaspoon) of cream cheese or peanut butter inside the toy, smeared along the inner surface to keep things low calorie yet irresistible
- Experiment with freezing or microwaving the contents to make a little bit go a long way (picture a tablespoon of oozing mozzarella on the inside of a Kong---much more challenging for your pup)

 To make a Pupsicle, block the tiny hole of a Kong with some cheese and place the otherwise empty Kong, large hole up, in a coffee mug. Fill the Kong with broth and place in freezer. You can also partially fill it and, as it freezes, add treats and another layer of broth so the puppy finds surprises and challenges as he licks away.

Chewing Things Outdoors

Try not to freak out too much when your puppy chews on a stick or pinecone outside. Most puppies chew on them and the bits just fall out of their mouths onto the ground. It is generally no big deal. However, some puppy owners turn it into a big deal by pouncing on their puppy and cramming their hands down the puppy's throat every time he grabs a stick or leaf. This teaches the puppy that sticks must be super valuable, and so they'd better guard them from you, swallow them as fast as possible, or run away in a great game of keep away. Heavens, try not to create such a monster. If you're really worried the pup may have something in his mouth he shouldn't, trade him for a treat in your pocket. Then teach him to bring items to you on cue in case it happens again (see the Fetch section). Even simpler is to keep him occupied with a game when you're outside instead of letting him wander around and munch on things he shouldn't, like toxic plants.

Solving food puzzles allows your puppy to expend mental and physical energy and helps meet his natural need to chew. It will also automatically reward him for amusing himself with his own toys instead of for chewing on you or your things. Rewarded behaviors become stronger and more frequent. Hence, lying quietly with a rewarding chew toy will prevent or replace bad habits. Ahhhh…

Bold or Bashful?

Bold Puppy Tip: Make sure the puzzles are challenging enough for your puppy. Occasionally give him a really interesting project (under your supervision), like a stuffed Kong tied up with a clean rag or old t-shirt and then sealed up in a cereal or shoebox, or his meal hidden in a leftover pizza box. I know what you're thinking, but not to worry, when these items are presented clearly as a toy (for example, outdoors and having the puppy sit first) puppies do not make the leap that all pizza boxes should be chewed on.

Bashful Puppy Tip: Encourage your puppy to forage for his breakfast by tossing it out into the grass (in your fenced yard). Also use food-dispensing toys made of different materials to get him used to clanking sounds. Make the toys especially inviting by putting something gooey (like peanut butter) on the *outside* of the toy to help get him started. Just tether him on a spread-out beach towel or sheet so clean up will be easy.

Chapter 12

Puppy Biting

You may be asking yourself, "Good grief, what is with all the biting? Is it normal?" The truth is that normal behavior in puppies 5 months and younger includes a lot of biting, whether social or exploratory. But it can be awfully painful for humans, what with our wimpy, thin skin at the mercy of those needle sharp teeth. Fortunately we can instill in the pup alternative choices that still meet his normal behavioral needs.

The following will help you prevent puppy biting and strategically reward alternative habits. Bad habits develop quickly, so if you implement the suggestions below and your puppy is still biting at your hands and feet after a few days, get customized help from a trainer. Don't wait. There is no reason you or your family should endure teeth marks all over your hands and forearms. The solutions below really work if you commit to them consistently. You should see results in under a week (fortunately good habits develop quickly, too).

Solutions For Socially Motivated Biting (The Puppy's Attempt To Get You To Interact)

If your puppy bites your hands when you pet him:

- Attempt snuggle time only when the pup is already pretty relaxed or even drowsy. Anything else is inviting a bite fest.

- Before you ever settle in with the pup or get down on the floor with him, hold a plush toy twice the size of

your puppy's head. The pup can bite on the toy while
you pet him or her. Should the pup miss the toy and bite
your hand, yelp once, stand and silently leave the room
with the toy. Return after 15 seconds and try again (this
usually works after three days of being consistent, and
sometimes after just a few repetitions).

- Play with the toy attached to a line that you drag
  along the floor/ground to keep teeth at a distance.
  Keep the toy touching the ground to prevent your
  pup injuring himself by leaping, twisting and landing
  funny.

- Teach the puppy fetch, find it and come-when-called
  games so you can interact in constructive ways.

If the puppy bites when you wrestle with him, pet his face, tussle
his ears, or pat him on the head:

- As soft as that widdle puppy head is, this kind of touch
  explicitly invites biting. Don't do it. Instead, always pet
  the puppy gently on the chest/under the chin.

- No wrestling. Wrestling will sabotage a lot of important
  skills the puppy needs to get along well in the world,
  like accepting being touched, restrained, reached for and
  calmly patted. Opt for a game of tug instead (see Tug
  section for correct way to play).

- Puppies try to get other puppies to bite and play with
  them by touching each other's faces and ears, so stick to
  calm petting under the chest or you will be asking your
  pup to bite your hands! It is not fair to ask the puppy in
  dog language to bite you, and then reprimand him for
  doing so.

If your puppy bites your clothes (bathrobe, skirt, pant leg,
superhero cape) when you walk past:

- Dangle a rope toy at teeth-level as you pass (not after the
  puppy bites at you, but preemptively). You can keep a few
  of these toys throughout the house so they'll always be

handy (they are cheap, plus you can make them out of old blue jeans). The pup will direct the biting onto the dangling toy.

- Bowl a treat out behind you as you pass; when the pup catches up to you after eating the treat, offer another treat at puppy nose-level (this is great preparation for leash manners, too).

- Teach your puppy to do a sit-stay as you walk by, and then offer a big reward. This is very easy to teach (see the Sit On Cue section) and, if you're consistent, will become your dog's habit when he is excited. Aren't you the stealthy owner?

If your puppy bites your leg, clothes or leash when you walk with him on leash:

- Dangle a rope toy at teeth-level. Do this automatically, rather than in response to biting.

- Bowl a treat out behind you; when the pup catches up to you after eating the treat offer another treat at puppy nose-level or next to your shoe. Repeat.

- If you need to re-group because he is biting at you or the leash like crazy, hold the leash straight out to the side momentarily (always allowing four paws on the ground) and wait for your puppy to calm down. Be ready with the toy or a treat to redirect his attention so he doesn't just go back to the biting.

- If your pup vigorously bites at his leash, the easiest solution is to ignore it for 10-15 seconds, as nearly all puppies will let go of the leash and move on to something else. Short puppy attention spans come in handy at times like this! If you make a federal case out of it, you could be creating an unnecessary showdown. If that doesn't work, as a last resort stop and act like a mannequin (no interacting). Gently, slowly guide the leash slightly skyward so the pup's chin is pointing upward (just slightly, all four paws should be touching the ground). That interrupts the game and isn't as fun as biting and tugging, so most puppies drop the habit provided you replace it with a rewarding one (like treats for walking by your side).

 Some puppies walk along gently holding the leash in their mouths. As long as they are not chewing the leash up, yanking on it, or biting their way up the leash toward your hand, this is no big deal. It can even be kind of cute.

If your puppy bites your kids' feet as they dangle over the edge of a chair or sofa or while they're getting ready for school:

- Time your puppy's meals so he can eat from a long-lasting food puzzle during such times. That will keep the pup's mouth and brain appropriately occupied and also instills the habit that sometimes we all sit quietly together. This prevents the rewarding feeling that comes from the kids' big reactions to the biting, plus it strongly rewards a new alternative. Keep stuffed puzzles in the freezer so you can grab one whenever you need it.

If your pup bites shoelaces or feet:

- Usually this happens at excitable times of day. Identify those times, then, just before that time of day, before the biting starts, tether your puppy to a nearby piece of furniture and provide an edible chew toy *before* he gets bored and starts going for feet. Engaging the pup with toy-on-string works, too. Just make sure you invite him to use the toy before he gets interested in your laces, or you'll be rewarding him for having chewed them!

Solutions For Exploratory Biting (The Puppy's Attempt To Learn About The World By Putting His Mouth On Everything)

Chewing on rug, table leg, sofa, plants, paperwork, clothing items:

- Puppy proof a room or two (nothing below 3 feet is safe).

- Prevent access to other rooms by keeping the doors of other rooms closed or using an exercise pen, baby gate or a crate.

- Make sure your pup has access to toys of different textures that she likes (see below).

Not chewing on a toy you've bought:

- Try other toys. The most engaging toys are usually those that are edible, or have a food component. Use peanut butter, cream cheese and/or kibble with hollow washable toys like Kong, Squirrel Dude, Twist n Treat, and puzzle balls to engage your pup.

- Rotate the toys every few days to keep them interesting to the pup. Works like a charm!

- Do not shove or wiggle toys into your puppy's face; this is a deterrent to play. Instead, wiggle the toy along the ground away from the pup to entice him to follow it.

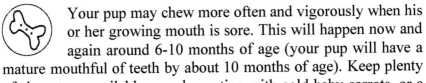 Your pup may chew more often and vigorously when his or her growing mouth is sore. This will happen now and again around 6-10 months of age (your pup will have a mature mouthful of teeth by about 10 months of age). Keep plenty of chew toys available, supplementing with cold baby carrots, or a rope toy or old washcloth that you've wetted, wrung out, and frozen. These cold treats bring relief, which equals less chewing on you and your things.

If it seems like your puppy is doing nothing but biting, and you basically just want to cry out of sheer frustration:

1.   He is likely trying to tell you he needs much more mental and physical exertion each day. Take him to a new place daily, ideally fenced in or with a long line, and let him run his little buns off (that is much different that jogging or intensive fetch, which is repetitive and concussive and can injure him). Feed his meals as food puzzles so he has to use his brain and body to get his food. Wear your puppy out a bit, physically and mentally, and he likely won't go all shark-attack on you.

2.   Let him wear a dragline or a leash indoors every day for a week or two. That way if he just starts going to town on you with his razor sharp chompers, you can stand on the leash with it very short or hold it out to the side until he is finished (all puppy paws touching the ground), direct him to his crate or exercise pen, or hand him to the nearest passerby (kidding!).

To teach your puppy not to bite your hands, avoid old methods that involved sticking things into or around the puppy's mouth or hurting or intimidating him with your hands. Hindsight is 20/20: Those physically punitive methods come with fallout, such as teaching puppies to be wary of human hands coming at them. You need your puppy to be trusting of your hands for daily care, for veterinary appointments, and for safety around your kids and you.

I know the biting can be painful and frustrating. But the above methods work, and pretty quickly (under a week), or I wouldn't recommend them. If you need a break, take one: crate or tether your pup with an edible chewy, do something relaxing for yourself, and then review your strategy from the list above. If you just can't take it anymore, get a reward-based trainer to help you. It's worth it and will save you headaches in the long run.

Bold or Bashful?

Bold Puppy Tips: Bold puppies can be pretty, er, extroverted with their biting. My advice is not to let your pup out of his confinement area without first asking yourself: "What is my plan to prevent biting at me?" and be ready to use the things above that are working for you. That normally does the trick.

Do not make any excuses for the pup if you are playing or touching appropriately, yet you still feel those teeth. Instantly yelp and leave. He will catch on that his human playmate prefers no teeth and will learn to adjust. If you're consistent, it works in just a few days.

Bashful Puppy Tip: Bashful puppies usually catch on to the prevention approach super fast; it's wonderful! Be consistent about offering a plush toy and chew toys and you should be in good shape. Sometimes three yelp-leave sequences are all it takes to show them the ropes. If anything, you may need to build your shy puppy's confidence around hands, for which I recommend teaching a nose touch and working on the body handling exercises.

Chapter 13

Feeding Routine: How, When, What And Where To Feed Your Puppy

For puppies under 5 or 6 months of age, most veterinarians recommend feeding three meals a day. You can switch to two meals a day around 6 months of age and stick to that for the life of your dog. A feeding routine can provide much-needed structure for your dog at times when life gets more unpredictable (you have a baby, move, or change work schedules, for example). Some puppies get an upset stomach by morning if they go to bed with an empty stomach, which is a nice excuse to feed them a little biscuit at bedtime. Your puppy should have access to fresh water; check with your vet to see if it's okay to remove it shortly after suppertime for overnight housetraining purposes.

Feed a high quality food, because healthier ingredients and fewer fillers mean smaller, less frequent piles of poop. (Woo hoo!) What this boils down to is that you should avoid foods that use ingredients listed as by-products, "meal" (like "chicken meal") and corn as the top ingredients. Stick to foods with whole meat sources and whole grains as the top ingredients. Particularly if you have a large breed or a toy puppy, check with your veterinarian for special recommendations.

Always feed your puppy in locations where you need to establish a very happy association, like inside the crate or exercise pen. If the puppy needs to feel more at ease with anyone in the family, that is who should feed him for a week. If he needs more confidence around strangers, enlist friends and neighbors to help and have them arrive, puppy food already in hand, at mealtimes. (Then invite them to dinner or send them home with cookies you've baked.)

Newsflash! Dogs do not need to eat out of bowls. They need to express their normal behaviors like chasing, biting and foraging. The more you meet your puppy's needs in a way that works for you, like mealtime, the less he will need to express chasing and biting your possessions as the targets. Therefore use the puppy's meal for a quick training or body handling session, feed the meal from a food puzzle, or hide it for him to find. All of these provide much-needed mental stimulation. Use a store-bought treat dispensing toy or just cut some holes in an empty water bottle for the same effect (first throw away the lid and little plastic ring, and supervise if you're using the empty water bottle).

Consider feeding your pup during your own mealtime. It will keep him occupied and he won't develop bad habits like bothering you at the table.

Have your puppy sit for each meal. This teaches self-control in the midst of excitement, which is a skill your pup will need his whole life. It also prevents barking, jumping, whining, lunging and other unpleasant mealtime behaviors that other dog owners have. See the section on training Sit On Cue. It should take just a day or two for your puppy to offer you lovely sits, then you can incorporate it into mealtime. Cue your puppy to sit or just hold the food puzzle at your waist (that in itself will likely get him to sit). Lower the meal puzzle to the floor as long as your pup remains sitting. Then praise and release with "ok!" so the puppy can move toward the puzzle. If the puppy starts to get up as you're lowering the toy, say nothing, just cease all downward motion of the meal. Be very quiet. Just pause and the pup will sit. Reward this by simply continuing to lower the toy. Repeat as necessary. Most pups figure this out in about three repetitions. Be patient. Say nothing. Let him work it out and ultimately that will improve understanding and lead to true mastery. That mental exertion will make him much more pleasant to be around later, because you'll have taught him how to work through feeling frustrated and use his brain to problem-solve.

Do not allow babies or children of any age to approach the puppy when he is eating. This will allow your pup to feel relaxed rather than defensive while eating, and keep your child safer with other dogs, too. Do not let other pets approach or otherwise bother your puppy (and vice versa) during mealtime. Just use a crate, exercise pen or baby gate.

Well-meaning humans think they are doing a good thing by "messing with" the puppy's food or food puzzle while he is eating. They think they are teaching the pup to accept human hands near his food. Unfortunately, if you do that you might teach a perfectly normal puppy that people do annoying things when he has something valuable. That can lead to defensive behavior like biting. Instead, teach your puppy to feel relaxed about having his meal interrupted. Approach him, take the food puzzle, praise as you hand the puppy a much, much better food item than what he had, and then immediately return the food puzzle or bowl to him. Do this just a few times a week. This teaches him that if someone should need to take his food away, a happy surprise is in store for him. (Wouldn't you just love it if someone took your chocolate chip cookie away, told you how great you are, handed you a slice of chocolate lava cake a la mode, and then gave you your cookie back?)

If your pup does not finish all of his food, do not leave it out for him to graze on. Anything he has not eaten in 10 minutes should be taken up for a later meal. Otherwise you will wreak havoc with your house training. Plus, if he's ever not feeling well and loses his appetite, you will know right away and be able to report to his veterinarian when he last ate.

There is no delicate way to put this: don't let your puppy get fat. Ask your veterinarian how to assess your pup's body condition and how to help him grow into a well-proportioned dog. Overweight dogs have health problems, are uncomfortable because it's harder for them to stay cool, and have much more strain on their joints. Your dog is counting on you to keep his svelte figure right from the beginning.

Bold or Bashful?

Bold Puppy Tip: Consider using a good 2/3 of your puppy's meals as a training opportunity. In place of official treats for teaching sit, loose leash walking, go to your place, or come, take 5-10 minutes and use the puppy's food as rewards for working on those skills.

Bashful Puppy Tip: If your pup is bothered by unexpected sounds, use gradually noisier meal dispensing toys so he will develop a happy association with loud things. The pup will cause the toy to make a loud sound in order for the meal to come out. The Treat Stick is made of hard plastic, as is the Buster Cube, so you could work up to those from something made of rubber like a Kong. Another idea is to start on carpet (or carpet remnant in his crate) and when the pup is at ease with that, move to a hard floor.

Part III
Life Lessons to Teach Your Puppy

Chapter 14

Play And Exercise

I long to be able to do the following experiment to prove how crucial exercise is to raising a well-behaved puppy: I make a training plan for a family to stop their dog's unwanted behaviors like jumping up, counter surfing, bolting out the door, chewing on forbidden objects, begging at the table or barking when confined.

I then clone the family and dog, and the cloned family with the same dog problems lives next door, but instead of a fancy pants training plan, that family changes only one thing: they meet their dog's daily exercise needs.

I bet myself a zillion dollars that the cloned family who meets their dog's exercise needs sees the same improvement in the dog's behavior as the family using training interventions. In short order, I would be a zillionaire. Plus, not only is the exercise family pleased with their dog's calmer state, they are all a lot happier because they are having fun with the dog, their dog is healthier, and they won't ever see the future difficult behaviors that will undoubtedly crop up for the family of the first dog.

Exercise is that important. It can have a big enough impact that, with some dogs, you can skip formal training altogether. For most dogs, choose from the suggestions for play, socialization and training in this book to provide a balance of mental and physical exercise.

Type And Amount Of Exercise To Provide Your Puppy

For really baby puppies under 3 months old, the activity of taking them to new places and romping with them in the yard after their potty breaks is usually plenty. Train the initial steps for learning fetch and walking politely on leash so that those skills will be installed when you really need them in just a few weeks.

For puppies 3 months and up, you can mix in casual leash walks and fetch with the above. Zooming around in a fenced yard or in a big field on a long line are good options. Play daily come-when-called games.

Puppies nearing adolescence (which starts around 6 months of age) should get several 15-20 minute play sessions a day of a mix of fetch, tug, running around, or walking on a soft surface like grass.

Dogs one year and older nearly always do best with two 30 minute aerobic exercise sessions a day. A nonchalant stroll around the neighborhood stopping at every blade of grass will not cut it, but rather you should aim for a moderately vigorous activity like trotting briskly beside you or running after a ball.

Balance out things your dog likes to do with things you like to do, and you'll both end up enjoying it. If you enjoy it, you'll be likely to do it every day.

Healthy Play

- Most veterinarians recommend waiting until your dog is at least a year old before engaging in repetitive, concussive activity like long, steady walks or jogs in which the dog is going trot-trot-trot for half an hour or more. It can put serious strain on growing ligaments and bones, resulting in injury later on. Unstructured, self-limiting movement like romping around, playing come-when-called games, "find it" games, or some fetch mixed in is best. Please ask you veterinarian what is best for your dog.

- Keep your puppy hydrated. Especially in warm weather, it is important to provide fresh water during activity. There is even a small water bottle you can buy that has a handy clip to attach it to your waistband, with a hinged bowl that allows your dog to drink. Give your pup a potty opportunity before coming back inside the house.

- Keep the play area clean of feces.

- Play with another dog is fine, but rarely is it aerobic. Plus, relying on it as a way to wear your puppy out can also create a dog who is too obsessive about dog play and doesn't give you the time of day when other dogs are around. At this tender age, let your puppy play with dogs you know who will teach your pup good habits. Usually that means an older dog who can show the pup a balance between play and down time.

- Do not wrestle or rough house with your puppy. Limit rowdy play to that which your pup directs onto a big plush toy tied to a string. This prevents a lot of bad habits like biting hands, fear of hands, biting at clothes, jumping up, avoiding restraint and the like. If you both like raucous games, see the sections on tug and recall games.

- Do not take your puppy to a dog park. It is too risky because you don't know the other dogs or how their behavior will affect your impressionable youngster. It would be like dropping your toddler off at the corner and hoping for the best. Maybe the other kids are nice and will show him the ropes. Maybe not so much. Also, in my experience dog owners rarely keep an eye on their dogs, preferring instead to cluster together and chitchat while their dog bullies someone or is being bullied. It is just too much of a free-for-all for a young pup (and it's no so great for an older dog, either).

  This is not going to dissuade some of you from going. Before you leave home, download the Dog Park Assistant app for your phone. If you still can't resist, at least go at a low-traffic time of day, let the dogs meet first with the fence between them (rather than letting the dogs charge your pup in a mass "greeting") and once you're inside the gate, keep moving. Walk all along the periphery the whole time, don't stand still and watch. Leave if anything makes you uncomfortable (regardless of what others may say). Really, your puppy is much better off if you make a play date with others you already know or could meet through your veterinarian. Puppy matchmaking, anyone?

Day care and boarding fall into the same category. If you need to leave your pup for a long stretch, arrange for your pup to stay with a friend, neighbor, or in-home sitting service. You may not be able to undo unnecessarily stressful events you could have prevented during the socialization period, so it's better to err on the side of your pup being happy in your absence.

Goodall Games

How can you know what your pup likes to do? You may find it helpful to play what I call Goodall Games with your puppy. These are named after the primatologist Jane Goodall, who quietly observed animals and let them teach her what they liked to do. Watch your puppy and notice whether he likes to use his nose a lot, if he prefers to rummage around in the bushes, chase bugs, dig holes, or grab at sticks and vines. Left to his own devices, without you encouraging him, what does he like to do? Take that information and make a game out of it. For example, I noticed my little dog enjoys rummaging around in the bushes. So I started hiding her toy in the bushes (making it super easy at first and letting her watch where I placed it) and lo and behold she became interested in fetch. The more I made the toy land in the bushes, the happier she was to hunt it down and bring it back to me for a reward. If your pup likes to chase bugs, you could mimic this by playing with a toy on a string; pull the string and make the toy hop and fly around.

Zippy Fast Recall Game

This game is an easy, fun way to exercise your puppy. It also instills in your puppy a strong reflex when he hears the word, "Come," to whip toward you and charge in your direction. This is also a wonderful game for children to play and is a great way to get a reluctant retriever started on playing fetch.

You will need treats that contrast with the color of the ground or floor you are working on. You'll also need a fenced in area or to stand on a long, thin leash line.

This is a fast moving game, so your treats must be pre-cut, small and soft, not crumbly or crunchy (macaroni noodles cooked in broth work great for playing on a darker surface). We don't want to slow the dog down by requiring a lot of chewing or hunting for crumbs. It could just create utter chaos, you know?

You will be tossing treats along a straight path, to the right and to the left of you, with you standing midway between the two treat landing spots. Like so:

Treat Landing Spot   You   Treat Landing Spot

Step One

Hold a few treats in both hands. Crouch or sit down and allow the pup to sniff the treats. Be silent or you will distract him.

Step Two

With an underhand motion as though you're bowling, toss the first treat out only 2 feet to your right. The pup will go out to get it. (He might be slow, that is normal at first.)

Step Three

At the moment the pup takes the treat in his mouth say, "Come!" Say the word once, and once only. Say it in a bright, cheerful voice, as though you are the Magic Treat Provider.

Step Four

Your puppy will turn back toward you and when he does, he should see you already bowling the next treat off to your left. Make sure he sees that arm motion. He will run past you to get treat #2.

Repeat a few times, but always end before the dog gets bored.

At first your puppy may not run. In fact, he may even be quite pokey about lifting his head up from eating the first treat. But lo and behold! After just a few repetitions, he will whip his head toward you when he hears "come!" and then automatically come flying toward you zippy fast.

Hints:

- With small puppies, squat down and stay there until they have the hang of it.

- As your pup gets the idea, increase the distance of the tosses.

- If you can time it right and it doesn't blow your mind, feel free to say, "get it" as your pup notices the bowled treat and heads toward it. This could help later with fetch, but it's not crucial so don't sweat it.

- Occasionally follow a "come!" by several treats fed directly from your hand instead of tossing another treat.

- Gently grasp the collar as you reward with the treats; this helps the puppy enjoy being reached for when he comes to you. Feed below your knee level to prevent jumping up.

- Always end with the last "come!" being followed by several treats fed directly from your hand, plus lots of cheerful praise.

Bold or Bashful?

Bold Puppy Tip: If all the excitement leads to grabby behavior to snarf the treats from your hands, just automatically (not after he's been grabby) place them by your toe for your pup to eat, and work on the sharky behavior separately, when your puppy is calmer.

Bashful Puppy Tip: Throw very short distances at first, maybe only 1 foot. You can even throw just one direction for the first few throws until your pup looks confident about charging away from you to grab the treat and then running back toward you.

Leash Training for Lovely Walks

A leash walk should be an exercise in partnership: it allows you and your dog to get some exercise, fresh air, and sensory stimulation as you maintain a conscious and respectful connection while moving along together. Or it can be like waterskiing, but without the water, as you hold on for dear life every time your dog plows toward a tempting distraction. Some puppies plant themselves like mules instead of walking along with you.

A medium-sized or large dog can injure your shoulder or hand if he's in the habit of pulling on leash. A small dog can injure himself by pulling against his trachea as you walk. A tight leash also causes problems with body language toward other dogs, and makes it hard for you to communicate with your dog if he is excited or distracted by something.

Therefore, for your well being as well as your dog's, make it a priority to teach your puppy to walk with you on a slack leash, by your side, keeping up with you from the beginning. Trust me, it can be a real bear to try to solve a leash pulling or a lagging-behind problem that is already established. Most people just don't have the time or patience. So it is worth it to prevent leash problems from developing. Starting today, commit to teaching him the right way to walk on leash. Let's get started!

The Right Equipment: Collars And Leashes And Harnesses, Oh My!

Choose a flat buckle collar or a limited slip ("martingale") collar. Adjust the collar so that no more than two of your fingers fit flat between it and your puppy's neck. This prevents him inadvertently twisting or backing out of it. Monitor the sizing as your puppy grows and buy a larger collar as needed.

 Your puppy's ID tags should always be attached to his collar (even if he's microchipped). To avoid jingling or the tags getting caught on things, use the Collar Tag by Boomerang.

Good news! You will not need a choke chain, pinch collar or shock collar to train your puppy. Thankfully there is no longer any need to use pain and intimidation now that there are other effective methods. (You might still see mean-looking collars in a store, or might be pressured by someone to use them. But the same can be said for cigarettes, and that does not make taking up smoking the best idea.)

Use a 4-6 foot leash rather than an extendable or retractable leash until your pup is well trained to walk by your side (this prevents confusion). You can switch once he has good habits. In the meantime, use a lightweight polyester line if you'd like him to be able to romp around in unfenced places and still keep him safe and legal.

From this day forward, this will be your Polite Walking Equipment. The collar and leash will predict for your pup a chance for rewards at your side, and no opportunity for pulling. So it is important to be consistent and use this equipment only when you are prepared to deliver rewards. Dogs form strong associations with hints in their surroundings, like a certain collar, that predict whether a situation will be rewarding.

What if you need to take the pup out for a quick potty, visit the vet, or get from your car into puppy class? At first those will not be ideal scenarios in which to coordinate rewards with polite leash walking. And that is okay. Just avoid spoiling the association of the flat collar with polite walking by using a front attachment harness (the leash snaps onto a ring at the front of the puppy, at his chest). The puppy won't be able to pull very much, if at all, and you will maintain the strong association with the collar that it is rewarding to stay by your side.

 Do not use a harness that has the leash attachment point on the puppy's back; this will only make it easier for him to lean forward and pull like a sled dog. That's the opposite of your goal! Use a front attachment harness instead.

The Right Rewards

Use soft (not crumbly), tiny, quick-to-swallow treats that are highly visible on the ground. The puppy needs to be able to spot the treat instantly and eat it without stopping or hovering for crumbs. Soft Buddy Biscuits for a light surface or macaroni cooked in broth for a dark surface are great options.

If you are using a toy, choose one that you can deliver yet still maintain possession of. Examples are a rope toy you can hold one end of, a plush toy or a squeaky toy with a long tail, or a ball on a rope that you can dangle into correct position.

Praise is very rewarding for some pups. Keep it calm enough to encourage calm behavior, and cheerful enough so you won't be confused with a military marching unit.

Do not pat your puppy on top of the head. As primates, we are very inclined to reach our hands out and pat, but most dogs and puppies do not like it (they show their discomfort by turning away, flicking their tongues, backing away, yawning, or even biting at our hands). However if you pet under the dog's chin or on his chest he'll likely lean in for more. It's like magic!

Walking Step-By-Step

You will be teaching your puppy how rewarding it is to walk by your side. If you make it consistently rewarding for your puppy to seek out your side, then that is where he will walk. Presto!

First, decide the side of you body you want your pup to default to. The right side is usually best, so that when you are in public your pup will be on the outside of your body and not have ready access to other dogs, baby strollers, or other passersby. If you are a jogger and plan to run against traffic with your dog, however, it is safer for your dog to be on your left, a bit further from oncoming traffic.

Second, begin in a distraction free place indoors (you will add distractions as you make progress). Carry your handful of treats in your right hand so you can easily reach down to reward your pup at your right side. Your leash will eventually be held in your left hand, but start without the leash to simplify things.

Now you are ready to begin. Your pup will likely be facing you, which is great. Start walking backwards, which will draw the puppy toward you. When his head is almost touching your right leg, say, "yes!" cheerfully and place a treat on the ground at the outside of your right shoe. At first reward each step, and as your pup gets the idea, add an additional step or two before rewarding. Work up (over a couple of sessions) to crossing to the other side of the room before saying "yes!" and delivering the reward near your right shoe. In a few days (yes, mere days!) you'll notice your pup snaps right into position, recognizing that when you start walking together, you backwards and he forwards, very good things happen near your right shoe.

Once you have this result, begin as usual. Then, before you reach the other side of the room, pivot your body by rotating your shoulders and hips to your left. Do not make a left turn, just pivot on the same travel path (practice without the puppy first; go back to 7th grade gym class in your mind's eye and imagine you are on a balance beam, or moving along a line painted on the ground). Once you have pivoted you will both be facing the same direction. Reward by your right shoe as usual. By rewarding your pup near your right shoe from the very beginning, that is where he will continue to place himself, even when you turn to face forward together. It's like magic, but really it is the science of rewards.

Practice in hallways and all rooms of the house. When you change locations, be very generous with your rewards, at first going back to rewarding each step forward (you will want to skip this and show off how smart your puppy is, but don't do it). When it's perfect, start varying how many steps you walk before saying "yes" and rewarding. When you are both looking quite professional, add the leash.

 It might sound goofy, but practice first without your puppy for best results. Everything will go smoother once you bring your pup into the picture, because you'll already be good at coordinating your treat delivery, walking and pivoting.

Bold or Bashful?

Bold Puppy Tips: Change directions frequently. This keeps your pup thinking, moving, and driving toward that reward spot near your right shoe.

Teach your pup to sit every time you stop. This gives him something to concentrate on rather than reverting to attention-seeking behaviors like jumping up or grabbing your pant leg. See the Sit On Cue section and start cuing the sit just before you bring your right foot in line with the left. He will catch on crazy fast and start sitting automatically. Brilliant!

Bashful Puppy Tips: Use the Nose Touch to get your puppy excited about keeping up with you. Offer your hand as a target low and by your right ankle. When he bops your hand, say, "yes!" as usual and feed the treat from the target hand, then continue on. This will instill happy confidence and make stopping or scratching at his collar less likely.

Watch where you're going; this will prevent you from looming over your pup or drifting into his space. You may find it helpful to aim for an object like a chair or a tree to keep your travel path away from that of your puppy.

Rein In Trouble

Get help from a professional trainer if you observe any of the following behaviors so that you can nip them in the bud before they become habits:

- Mouthing your hands or arms when putting on or adjusting the leash or collar

- Running away from you, with or without hiding, when you get out the leash or collar or attempt to put it on

- Any of the following when you touch the collar any time during the day: Whipping her head around at you (open or closed mouth); mouthing, snapping at, or biting your hands; freezing; giving a stare or glassy-eyed look; growling

- Tugging hard with teeth on the leash for more than about a second

- Biting/tugging at/shaking/climbing up/grabbing and re-grabbing the leash closer to your hand

- Straining towards adults, children or dogs and doing any of the following: whining, lunging, front feet off ground, barking, snarling (lifting lip), growling, putting the hair up on the neck, back, and/or tail

- Attempting to charge after cars, squirrels, birds or other animals (silently or barking)

- Turning toward you and lunging, snapping or biting you if he cannot reach the above listed targets

- At the sight of other people, dogs or objects, any of the following: cowering, shrinking away, tail tucked, trembling, hiding behind you, pupils dilated

Find It

This game gives your dog an outlet for his natural scavenging talents (meaning he'll be less likely to hunt down your possessions), can be mentally and physically tiring, is ideal when inclement weather prevents outdoor exercise, gives your puppy something to do in the veterinary waiting room or puppy class while waiting his turn, and is appropriate for kids to play under adult supervision. He'll have the hang of it in about three sessions.

All you need is your puppy wearing a collar and a handful of smelly, non-crumbly treats (like macaroni cooked and tossed in garlic powder or pieces of your puppy's regular meal).

Session One

Step One

Hold your treats in one hand and your puppy by the collar in your other hand. Place one treat about 2 feet in front of your puppy. He should be staring at it with great intensity (if not, move it closer).

Step Two

Say, "Find it!" (But do not say your puppy's name, or you will confuse him at best and at worst inadvertently reward him for ignoring his name and diving toward a distraction in the environment).

Step Three

After you have finished uttering the Find It cue (not while you are saying it), release your hand from the pup's collar so he can surge toward the treat and eat it.

Repeat with 5-10 treats, ideally in different locations in the room or house. Don't worry if your puppy seems slow at first, he will get it. Ta da! You have completed the first session. Wait a few hours to a day and go on to session two.

 Do not release the puppy if he is struggling to get free of your restraint or you'll be inadvertently rewarding having a fit. Just silently wait him out and release the moment he is still again.

Session Two

Repeat the above, but this time in Step One you will set the puppy up two feet away from a chair leg or coffee table leg. Instead of placing the treat in plain view, place it just behind the furniture as he watches.

Say, "Find it," and then, separately, let go of the collar.

Be patient and let the pup sniff around for the treat. Just be silent and watch how he uses his nose. It's pretty cool.

Repeat 5-10 times, setting the pup up about two feet from various pieces of furniture, tucking the treat behind a door that is ajar, or setting it just around the corner of the next room. If your pup gets stuck, move the treat closer or back into view for a few repetitions, but do not bribe him with other treats or point madly at the hidden treat.

Session Three

Now you can make it more advanced by using a helper to hold the puppy by the collar while you hide the treat further away, or by tossing the treat to its hiding place.

Step One

Set the puppy up about five feet from the hiding place.

Step Two

Toss the treat (or have your helper hold the pup by the collar). After it lands out of sight say, "Find it."

Step Three

Release the pup to go hunt down the treat.

Repeat 5-10 times, setting the pup up further from the hiding place, putting or tossing the treat into the next room, or increasing the challenge by pretending to hide a decoy treats behind several coffee table legs and placing only one real treat.

Once your puppy masters these challenges you can practice playing Find It on leash (and then off leash) outdoors, while you're seated in a chair, with a toy instead of treats, and eventually even with your car keys if you're prone to misplacing them. Once you've taught your puppy a sit-stay (see the Sit On Cue section) you'll be able to cue your puppy to sit and wait while you hid the treat, then return to him and reward him with a treat for sitting, then cue him to Find It. Fancy.

Fetch

Playing fetch is a great way to exercise and spend time with your dog. It also provides an outlet for natural predatory behavior. Some dogs take to the game in no time. Others lose interest quickly, become distracted, or trot away with the ball once they've chased it down. And then there are the dogs who bring it back, but won't let you take it from them.

To solve all these problems, play a game called two-toy fetch. It can hook a reluctant retriever into playing fetch, and even get a ball hog into the habit of dropping the toy at your feet. It is based on the game of keep-away, which I am pretty sure dogs invented.

Your goal is to teach the dog to race back to you with the ball, quickly drop it, and take off after the next ball.

You will need two toys that are perfectly similar, so the dog won't prefer one to the other. A tennis ball and a squeaky ball are not similar enough; you must play with two identical toys (i.e. two of the very same squeaky balls). Keep these toys out of your dog's reach until it's time for fetch.

You pup should sit quietly to start the game. Thereafter, require no more sitting, just play. End the game while your puppy is still eager for you to throw the toy one more time. If that means you can only throw the ball twice at first, so be it! Always leave him hoping for more, thereby ensuring you can gradually increase the number of throws.

Here is the critical ingredient for success: you must be willing to make a total fool of yourself. You'll notice that starts right off the bat...

Step One

Excitedly introduce the dog to the two toys by holding them close to you and remarking on how wonderful they are. To pique your pup's interest, you may need to do this for a couple of days before ever throwing the toys. Never hold the toys up to your puppy's face; it is a common mistake and a sure-fire way to annoy the dog and turn her off of fetch.

Step Two

Position yourself in the center of a 15-foot area, like an indoor hallway to prevent your puppy from becoming distracted. If your pup is fairly toy oriented, try outdoors in a fenced-in area.

With an underhand motion as though you're bowling, throw the first toy out only 5 feet to your right. Technique is very important because a dog new to fetch needs to track the toy with her eyes; overhand throws usually cause the puppy to utterly miss the toss. After your first toss, the pup will run out to get it.

 If your pup has never shown any interest in any type of toy, before you play this game with toys, first play the Zippy Fast Recall Game.

Step Three

At the exact moment the dog takes the toy in her mouth, turn your back and run in the opposite direction, whooping it up over the second toy in your hand. Draw your pup's interest in it by tossing it skyward, sniffing it dramatically, and pretending to drop it. Really go for that Academy Award in Keep Away. This is the part that works like magic. I have never, ever seen this method fail to get any dog playing fetch.

 If you look over your shoulder, call your pup, coax him to you, face him, or otherwise show interest in him and his toy, you are sunk. Fake keep away is a sorry sight and your puppy will recognize it a mile away. Play keep away like you mean it!

Some dogs may need a few minutes of you acting like a real noodle, or you may need to start out in a very small space indoors like a hallway, but it always works. Inevitably, the dog will approach you with her ball, fascinated by the "better" one you have, and drop the one in her mouth.

Now, be ready. This is the moment that counts:

Step Four

When she drops her ball (even if she is not right at your feet at this stage), instantly say, "yes!" and begin the process again by throwing, underhand, ball #2. Off she'll go, after ball #2. While she heads for ball #2, quickly step on ball #1 (don't reach for it, step on it), then pick it up and reposition yourself in the center so you'll be ready to run away again. (Note: do not touch the puppy, feed a treat or praise her. Simply say, "yes!" and throw, or you risk confusing her with extraneous information. For best results keep up the adrenaline and focus on that ball!)

Over the course of a couple of weeks, you'll be able to throw the ball further. You won't need to run away or make such a big production out of it, because your dog will have figured out that the faster she brings the toy to your feet, the faster you will throw the "better" one. From then on, you can play with two toys or just one toy. If you start saying "get it" at that stage, just before you toss the toy, you'll be on your way to having a retrieve on cue.

The most important part is your Oscar-worthy performance. You must believe your toy is better, and show no interest in your dog until she drops her toy. If you can do that, your puppy can learn to play fetch with enthusiasm.

Tug

Dog owners sometimes admit to me that they play tug with their dog, but they always say it in hushed tones, as though they have been caught at something forbidden.

Sure, tug has a competitive component to it. But perhaps it is no more competitive than a game of fetch, in which a valued object has to be shared back and forth between the dog and the person. When you think about it, tug of war is a game that requires true cooperation. Without you, your dog cannot play it, and vice versa (you'd look silly trying!). In fact, tug of war can teach your dog to share with you (because you'll teach him "give" so you can gain instant control over the toy), how to get fired up and then calm down (because you'll reward his dropping it with a chance to restart the game, on cue), and that without you there is no tug, but with you, there is a lot of fun to be had (because you'll play with a special tug toy that you'll present, when you feel like it, as a reward for coming when called, just for fun, or on a rainy day instead of a longer walk).

Here are important pointers for successful tug:

- Generally speaking, tug is not as good a game for kids to play with their dogs as fetch is because of the many, quick decisions that have to be made. Plus, it is too physical a game for most kids to be able to control well.

- If your dog typically releases the toy and quickly re-grips it, so that he grabs it closer and closer to your hand as you play, I recommend you get some professional advice before continuing. He may be a little too competitive and need some customized rules for the game. (The same goes for dogs who get grabby with their fetch toys.)

- All those teeth, and the play growling that can accompany tug, might make you uneasy. If you don't enjoy that, or you're not sure whether your dog is just kidding around, then either find some other games to play or get some in-person pointers from a qualified trainer on how to make tug fun for both of you. Generally speaking, growling that appears random and intermittent, that accompanies loose body language, and that is higher pitched and sounds like its coming from your puppy's head is perfectly normal during a high-arousal game like tug. Growling that sounds low, from the belly, accompanied by stiff body language, multiple freezes or hard staring, and occurs in response to you reaching for the toy or a spike of intensity in the game, are serious enough signs that I recommend getting advice from a professional trainer.

- If your puppy already shows aggressive displays around objects he doesn't want you to take from him (this is called resource guarding), tug is unlikely to be a good game for him. But fetch could be dicey, too, since it also involves reaching for something your dog wants. So get professional assistance with that issue before settling on a game that's right for you.

- Make sure all four of your puppy's feet maintain contact with the ground at all times during tug. As tempting as it may be to lift his front feet or swing him around, doing either risks injury. Instead, hold the toy low and still, and let your puppy be the one to pull back and move his own head around how he chooses.

- Speaking of avoiding injury, use an underhand grip to engage your biceps and bend your knees. Keep your elbows close to your body and engage your core. This should help keep your back and arms from getting jerked around and will be even more helpful as your puppy gets bigger.

If you'd like to play tug with your dog but he's just not interested in toys, start by teaching him that toys are exciting by introducing fetch in a small room. Use lightweight, braided fleece toys like the Tuff E Nuff Tug that are the right size for his mouth, and drag them a few feet from him as though you were enticing a cat to play (do not wiggle the toy in front of his face; most dogs are put off by that). Above all, let him "win" and grab the toy out of your hand so that you can build his confidence in the game. Let him chase you around with the toy in his mouth. Keep sessions very short (1-2 minutes, tops) and end with him wanting to play more.

Teach "Give" And "Get It"

Once your dog has the hang of grabbing the toy, maintain hold of the toy but let it go slack as you present a treat. This will cause your pup to drop the toy. Just when she is about to release the toy to eat the treat, say, "give." After your pup spits out the toy reliably when she feels the tension leave the toy and she sees the treat (about 5-10 repetitions spread over a few sessions), reverse the order of events so that the word comes first, then the treat. Let the toy go limp (you may need to actually move the toy toward your pup to create that effect). Then say, "give" and wait a beat; your pup will likely drop the toy and then you can present the treat.

There, you are rewarding your puppy for giving up the toy on cue! Before long you can cue "give" and alternate feeding a treat reward with praise, or permission to grab the toy for more play, or another real-life reward, like a chance to eat supper or go for a walk. To teach the puppy some self-control around toys, turn away if the pup lunges for the toy and consistently say, "get it" when it's okay for the pup to grab the toy again (sitting patiently is a nice habit to reward by cuing "get it" and starting another round of tug).

Give tug a try! You and your pup will have a whole new way to enjoy each other.

Bold or Bashful?

Bold Puppy Tip: Break up the tug sessions with training exercises like sit, stay and come. Here's how: Play tug for no more than ten seconds at a time before cuing "give," and then ask for a still position, a trick, or call your puppy and take off running. Say "yes" and reward your pup by cuing "get it" for your pup to grab the toy for more play.

Bashful Puppy Tip: If your pup needs extra incentive to grab the toy even after trying the tips above, put treats into an old sock (knotted) or try using a Tuggit toy stuffed with treats. Also, be careful not to overwhelm your bashful pup with your own enthusiasm.

Dog-Dog Play

Your puppy needs to learn to play well and communicate effectively with other dogs. Otherwise he could turn into a pain in the patootie to walk on leash, whether because he is overly excited to play with every passing dog, or because he is lunging and barking out of anxiety or frustration.

The best way to ensure healthy doggie social development is to arrange meetings with dogs of different genders, sizes, and ages so that he learns to read the nuances of dog language from his elders and from his peers. "Leash aggression" towards other dogs that crops up as young dogs mature is fairly common, unpleasant for the dog, and a huge pain in the rear for the human to resolve. It's best to do what you can to prevent it.

 Work up to "chance" meetings with dogs your puppy already knows in the settings he will later encounter unfamiliar dogs, like the waiting room at the vet, your favorite walking paths, your neighborhood, and the parking lot of your favorite dog training school. About half the time, don't have them meet, but rather reward the pups generously for just quietly hanging out or passing politely on a loose leash. Ideally your pup will later think, "Hey, there's a dog I don't know, but I've practiced saying hello to my buddy Frank here, so I don't need to get worried or wild."

Play dates with older, friendly dogs you already know, ideally a few times a week, are most likely to work well. Your veterinarian or local puppy class may offer group play opportunities as well, provided they are carefully planned and supervised by an experienced, engaged professional who provides lots of troubleshooting help. Before you choose a puppy class, call ahead to arrange a chance to observe to make sure you see all of the following. The puppies should:

- Have structured meetings with new dogs and people preceded by clear instructions so the puppy rehearses desirable behavior with both dogs and people

- Practice coming to their person out of a group of dogs

- Calm down nicely between play periods

- Learn to focus on their person in the presence of the other participants

The puppy owners should learn what normal puppy play looks like and how to help their pups out if they need it. The class should not be a free-for-all. The instructor should match play partners carefully, use gates or a dragline on an individual pup if needed, and coach the owners when they need some assistance. The puppies should be spending most of their time calmly hanging out with their people, interspersed with planned visits with the other puppies or humans.

The goal should be for the puppies to leave the social time better than they arrived. They should have a good experience with the puppies and people they meet.

If all this is not provided in the class setting, and I really mean this, you are better off arranging your own play dates rather than attending a formal puppy class. It can lead to problems later if your puppy is matched with a roomful of equally inexperienced hooligans and a lackadaisical instructor.

So what should you look for in good dog play? What are signs of trouble and what should you do?

Good things to see when puppies play:

- Playing as though they are the mirror image of each other, or as though they are dancing a duet, whether they are wrestling, leaping or running

- Inefficient movements such as flopping around, showing exaggerated movements (like giant biting without pressure, or floppy tandem galloping)

- Reading the signals of the other puppy and adjusting accordingly (backing off if there is cessation of movement, trying again more gently, or trying to copy how the other puppy plays)

- Breaking off from play of their own accord to sniff, explore, rest, check in with a person, or get water

Problems brewing when puppies play together:

- Bullying behavior in which a dog relentlessly targets one or more dogs (which may include standing over them motionless, body slamming, rolling them, making them yelp or targeting a body part)

- Terrified behavior (tail tucked, trembling) from which a puppy does not recover, but rather cowers or hides

- Non-stop, obsessive play without breaking off on their own

- Consistent failure to read other dogs' cues and moderate intensity of play accordingly

- Drifting into true predatory mode, with the emergence of quiet, efficient movements. These include staring at and intensely stalking another dog (play signals will be absent. This occurs usually with older dogs and is not very common.)

- Misunderstandings arising from mismatched play styles, possibly leading to fights or feeling overwhelmed (for example, dogs like Labrador retrievers and pit bulls often engage in body slamming. A border collie may prefer to chase and be chased, and terriers may like to bite hard and wrestle.)

You should promptly interrupt such behaviors. Just step between the two puppies and each person should guide their dog by a leash in the opposite direction. Do not resume play between them. Rather, make sure that your pup has ample opportunity to interact with older dogs known to be patient and clear in their signals, so that only the right kind of play is rewarded with more play. Get the Dog Park Assistant phone app to view video examples. If you see any of these behaviors more than once in your puppy, consult with a qualified trainer or behaviorist. If you delay, your puppy could be on the road to developing serious anxiety or dangerous habits around other dogs. And that's nothing to play around with.

Chapter 15

Body Handling

Throughout your puppy's life, he will need to feel at ease with human hands touching him. If your dog does not readily accept body handling, you and others, including children, are likely at greater risk for bites. Out of respect and kindness it is only fair to prepare your puppy for all the body handling we humans need to do.

You and others will pat him to show affection, examine him if he has hurt himself, administer eye drops or ear medication, and groom him (including trimming his nails, bathing and toweling him off, and wiping his feet dry). Veterinarians and their assistants will weigh your dog, take his temperature, hold his leg still to take a blood sample, examine his entire body (including eyes, ears and teeth) and restrain him for various procedures over the years. Trying to distract him with treats will get them only so far, as I am sure they will attest.

Furthermore, your veterinarian will not be able to provide the same level of care she would if your dog was calm and still for examinations. Imagine the trouble your human doctor would have providing quality care for you if you kept dodging her hands, saying, "Don't touch me, it freaks me out!"

Despite folklore it is not sufficient to "mess with his feet" while you pet your puppy each evening. It may even create problems by annoying your puppy and teaching him to struggle when touched. Don't leave it to chance. Just as you teach your puppy to sit, come and where to potty, you need to teach him to feel genuinely happy about being handled and restrained.

And now for the good news! It takes only about 5 minutes a day to accomplish your goal of a puppy who is relaxed about restraint and body handling. Simply pair your body handling lessons with hand-feeding his dinner to create a pleasant association. It may only take a week or two for you to be able to work up to handling similar to that which he'll find at the vet.

Five Minutes A Day Keeps The Problems Away

The key is not to dive right into to tricky body areas that might agitate the pup (like his face or feet), but rather to touch the pup in places he's very comfortable with, very gradually blending into places that might make him uneasy. Proceed at the pace that avoids going beyond the pup's comfort level, lest you inadvertently teach him to feel upset about body handling. You know you're doing it right if he seems relaxed and happy because of the treats.

Step One

Measure your puppy's food out, but instead of putting it in a food puzzle for him, put it in a coffee mug and set it within reach of you on a table or chair. (If you think your puppy will take off, choose a small powder room or laundry room to limit his options.)

Step Two

Sit on the floor with the puppy. One hand will remain clean and will do the body handling; the other will deliver the meal a bit at a time.

Step Three

Choose an easy spot (like the ribcage). Hold your clean index finger on that spot for a count of one second. (Count in your head, "one-banana.")

Step Four

Say "yes!" to let him know that touch just earned him some food.

Step Five

Feed a small handful of his supper from your treat hand.

It all happens in three seconds: 1) touch and say "yes" 2) feed some kibble and 3) remove your touch hand. Avoid petting during this exercise so your puppy will get the message clearly as to what kind of touch is the tip-off for morsels of supper coming his way.

Work your way up to your puppy's back and down to his elbows, which will be about 10 distinct touches paired with handfuls of supper. Your first session is complete! At the next session, start incorporating his tail and ears, and so on. After a few suppers, you should be able to touch your pup anywhere for one second. That sound you hear is your vet contemplating that you might be the world's best puppy owner.

What To Do About Mr. Squirmy McSquirmyPants

Squirming at first is normal and an easy thing to work through. Here's how:

Let's assume the pup squirms or gets a little mouthy when you attempt to touch his paw.

First, make sure you are not actually grasping or holding any body parts yet, just touching for one second with your index finger.

Second, avoid reprimanding him, as he is just telling you it is too much for him, and that is information you need in order to proceed productively. (It is not "bad" behavior any more than it would be "bad" for a toddler to be afraid of getting a shot.)

Finally, touch an easy spot far from his paw (perhaps his back), say "yes!" and then deliver the food reward. Then, moving only slightly closer to the paw (like his shoulder or halfway down his leg), touch just briefly and reward. Gradually increase the proximity of your hand to his paw and the length of time your hand remains there. As you work on getting your hand closer to the paw, use table scraps that he can't resist, or cheese if he loves that. Tiny bits (the size of a small pea) are best for training as well as for maintaining your puppy's waistline.

The above instructions work for most puppies. If you feel your pup is a real wild child, instead of incorporating the body handling lesson into dinner time, choose a time of day when your puppy is typically about to drift off to sleep for a nap. If none of these suggestions work, get help from a trainer. If your puppy is reacting that strongly, it would be pretty easy to make things worse by troubleshooting on your own.

However, if all is going well, you are ready for the body handling big leagues! Start with just a few seconds and work up to being able to hold your index finger anywhere on your pup for a count of 7 seconds before giving him the treat. This includes each toe, his eyebrows, tail, cheeks, and ears. Then incorporate hugs that last 2 seconds and work up to 7 seconds. This mimics what the veterinary technician must do to restrain your pup. (It's a sort of hug-around-the-neck; reach under your puppy's neck, which will rest in the crook of your bent elbow.)

Add a brief head pat, hug or a kiss as a child might offer them, followed by a favorite treat. Most dogs object to the invasiveness of hugging and kissing (bites to children's faces are common as a result). It might help your dog tolerate this kind of touch if you train it as part of your body handling exercises. (See the Kids and Dogs section on appropriate alternative ways for kids to show affection.) It is more respectful and safer to pet a dog under the chin or on the chest, but your puppy will likely be on the receiving end of head patting, hugging or kissing at some point so it is a kindness to prepare him ahead of time.

Finally, begin to actually hold up a paw, his tail, his lip, and an ear.

When you can do that and your pup is relaxed, and you have the itch to really show off, add these elements:

- Practice on a slick surface (linoleum or hardwood floor).

- After a couple of days, carefully place your pup on a higher surface, like an ottoman, then a picnic table, and finally washing machine (with the door closed, wise guy!). For the first few days, cover the slick surface of the washing machine with a rubber bath mat for extra stability. Pay attention and hold your puppy at all times; do not allow your uncoordinated or adventurous pup to fall or jump off!

- When that's easy, remove the mat so your puppy experiences a slick surface, up high, similar to the exam table at the vet's office or the groomer's table.

- If all is going smoothly, have a neighbor or friend touch the puppy, "examining" his ears and tail, while you feed treats (first on the floor, then up higher).

- It is best to hook a thumb under your puppy's collar and hold his chest so you can easily steady him should he start to fall.

The Weekly Once-Over

After your initial body handling lessons, practice once a week with treats to maintain the association. The Weekly Once-Over is a great lifelong habit to get into to check for any bumps, changes, parasites or mats in your puppy's coat. It is also the perfect time to gently swipe your puppy's teeth with doggie toothpaste dabbed on a square of gauze as preparation for struggle-free tooth care.

Each week until your pup is about four months old, have a friend or neighbor do the Weekly Once-Over while you feed treats, so the pup learns to love being restrained and examined by others besides you.

With this approach, your puppy will welcome touch, restraint, and examination and will be on his way to enjoying visits to the veterinarian and groomer. When you are ready to introduce toenail trimming, treatments like ear cleaning, or the touch of a toddler, you will be ahead of the game. And you won't believe how popular your little fuzzbutt will be at the veterinary office; he will become a favorite patient because he will be a joy to work with and you will have peace of mind knowing he gets the care he needs.

How To Pick Up And Put Down Your Puppy

Teach your pup to enjoy being picked up and held by a variety of people by pairing it with treats. This is especially important if you have a very small dog who will likely be picked up by you and others throughout his life. Here's how: stand facing roughly the same direction as your pup. Scoop one hand or forearm under the puppy's rear end under his tail, place the other hand between his front legs (from behind the elbows) to support his chest. Then, as you lift him, bend at your knees and use your legs to stand up, not your back. Keep your elbows bent and draw the puppy very close against your body. (Never lift the puppy up under the armpits as though he were a child or a cat as this can injure him.)

To create a happy association, first lift the pup, and then present a treat (ask a helper to feed the treat). Always place the pup gently back on the floor, all four paws down at once like you're touching down a helicopter (do not let him jump or slide out of your arms).

 To transfer your puppy to someone else, always put him down first and then the other person should pick the pup up from the ground.

Nightmare puppy training alert! If your puppy struggles in response to restraint, examination or grooming and you put him down or stop what you were doing, you are rewarding the squirming and it will likely get worse. Wait until the puppy returns to being still and calm, then put him down. Next, choose an easier area to examine and work up gradually to the tricky spot, or lift the puppy only partially or briefly. Provide plenty of treats along the way.

 Children should not be allowed to lift or carry puppies. It makes most puppies miserable, teaches kids to treat puppies like playthings instead of individuals with feelings, and can injure the puppy. See the Kids and Dogs section for appropriate alternatives.

Bold or Bashful?

Bold Puppy Tips: As soon as you work through all of the above exercises, add more advanced body handling lessons (your veterinarian or dog trainer can help you learn to do these correctly):

Lifting onto a table
Using a brush and comb (for one minute before presenting a treat)
Introducing Pedi-Paws nail file or nail trimmers
Having ears cleaned (use a dry cotton ball)
Bathing
Pretend vet exam
Pretend veterinary restraint
Pretend grooming session (mist with spray bottle, run hair dryer on low nearby)
Holding by collar
Holding in arms
Brushing teeth
Touching with a neutral object such as a metal serving spoon (to mimic objects used by your vet, groomer, or a child who forgets the rules about not touching dogs with objects)

Bashful Puppy Tips: Do all of the above, plus teach him how to touch stranger's hands on cue. Use the Nose Touch discussed in the Training Skills section of this book. Your shy puppy will come right of his shell for handling by others if you teach him to bop his nose to a stranger's hand when presented with their flat palm. This works because it boosts his confidence by letting him have a little control over the situation, all the while creating a happy association with hands by making them part of a game.

Your helper must sign a blood pact promising not to attempt stealth petting before or after he has completed the nose touch. They will try it anyway because your puppy is irresistible, so after your puppy does his little nose touch to their palm, say "Yes!" and instantly reach in to feed him a luscious treat. Shamelessly lure him with the cookie towards you before they can get their mitts on him. It is important for shy puppies not to feel ambushed. Create predictable scenarios and trust will blossom.

Once your pup is having fun with the hand touch with helpers, incorporate the advanced steps above with helpers, and finally the list above, first with you and then with helpers. Keep sessions short and sweet and use extra special treats. It will be worth the effort for a lifetime of confidence with being handled and restrained.

Chapter 16

Socialization

New puppies are curious, inquisitive little sponges, soaking up experiences and information about the world. They are ready to develop lasting impressions, for better or for worse. In fact, it is widely held that they have a "critical period" of social development up until approximately age sixteen weeks, during which time they are especially open and sensitive to learning about things they'll encounter throughout their lives. Given this time window, the sooner you can start taking your puppy out into the world, the better.

Having said that, your puppy is not a blank slate just waiting to be ruined by you (personality, development and behavior are so much more complex than that), so don't let anyone guilt trip you or terrify you into paralysis. Just do the best you can with the parts you can control and don't leave them to chance, even as you recognize a lot of your puppy's development has to do with genetic and environmental influences beyond your control.

The Best Age To Introduce Your Puppy To The World

Most veterinarians now recommend early and frequent socialization opportunities, even if the puppy has not finished all vaccinations. Veterinarians who are board certified in behavior, in fact, say the risk of your puppy dying from exposure to a virus in puppy hood is far less likely than death from euthanasia due to behavior problems later on that might have been prevented through planned exposures to novel people, places, other animals, and things.

The American Veterinary Society of Animal Behavior states that puppies can attend puppy classes starting at 7-8 weeks of age. They say pups should receive a first deworming and one set of vaccines a week before they attend class. Puppies should encounter as many new people, dogs, and environments as possible. In other words, do not let outdated beliefs about puppy exposure to disease keep you from helping your puppy with what he needs most: happy exposure to things he'll need to cope with his whole life.

If you are uneasy about making the change to the new recommendations, I advise taking the pup with you and simply not setting him on the ground. You can keep him or her on your lap, in your arms, or on a huge blanket so the pup can take in the sights, sounds and people you encounter. Your vet may recommend you try to stick to locations where it's unlikely a lot of unvaccinated dogs have spent time.

Here are the most important reasons to take your pup out into the world with you as soon as you bring her home at 7 or 8 weeks of age. Doing so will provide a chance to:

- Create happy associations with the types of experiences your pup will need to take in stride as an adult

- Tire your puppy out. Mental stimulation is just as important as physical exercise. You'll be amazed how much calmer your pup is after a field trip or visiting with new people

- Get your puppy to the veterinarian's office in between vaccinations, just for fun so he looks forward to his other visits

- Teach your puppy how fun car rides can be

- Have a mildly stressful experience or two and bounce back from it, just like will occur throughout your dog's life

Puppy Field Trips

When you venture into the world together, the key is to create exposures that are truly happy experiences. Your job is to make sure your puppy is not merely exposed to new things, but rather that her little tail is wagging out of happiness most of the time you are out. To achieve this, don't stand by and watch your puppy. Be involved. Pair her interactions with others with a confident, upbeat attitude, along with plenty of treats (from you, not from the other person) and a favorite toy. If you are not sure what you're doing, it's ok, just try to exude happy confidence and keep the goodies coming. You and your puppy are emotionally connected and your attitude can help set the tone.

I don't recommend letting strangers pet your puppy until they agree to do so in a way that will most benefit the pup: i.e. only if the pup comes to them, and then only under the chin or on the chest. (If you see a cute puppy, or any dog, please ask the owner for permission before touching or interacting with their pooch.)

 Do not allow children to mob your puppy. It can teach your pup to feel overwhelmed around kids, and can teach the kids that the puppy's feelings are less important than their desire to pet him. Instead, instruct kids to take turns petting the puppy under the chin or on the chest. This can continue as long as he is approaching them and asking to be petted. When he has had enough and gets over stimulated or turns away, it's time to cheerfully thank the kids and move on. Next time aim for a shorter session or fewer kids.

Find Your Inner Rock Star (When Things Don't Go As Planned)

Not every person you meet will do it right, so if someone comes on too strong and your pup should need encouragement, be quick to say, "What a brave puppy!" in a happy tone, and if necessary be on your way. People do some wacky things, thinking they have mystical dog powers, and it never ceases to amaze me. They will even promise to follow your instructions and then change their mind. Stay upbeat for your pup's sake and move away the moment they do not follow your instructions or if your pup starts to look less happy.

If your puppy really balks or resists at any point, just take it as information that you need to back up and pair an easier step with some of his meal, praise and a favorite toy. It is best to create trust with your dog rather than fear. Therefore, allow him to explore at his own pace without pressure or coaxing. Be patient and upbeat and proceed when he's relaxed and playful again. Think of it this way: if the sight of a spider panicked you, I would not tell you to get over it and then put one down the back of your shirt. That is neither effective nor kind. Of course if your pup has a very strong reaction and does not bounce back, contact your dog trainer or class instructor so you can pick the best plan of action for your particular puppy. It may be a simple fix, and it's important not to wing it.

> If your puppy is hesitant to approach someone, do not try to talk the pup into it. Avoid saying things like, "It's okay! Go say hi!" as you probably sound a little embarrassed or unsure, which will not help the puppy. Do not try to get the person to feed the puppy a treat to bribe the puppy towards them. This is a band-aid and can backfire. Instead, let the puppy decide if and when she wants to approach someone, then celebrate with praise and treats. Next time use the Bashful Puppy Tips at the end of this section.

Choose The Right Experiences For A Well-Rounded Puppy

Introduce to your pup the sounds, sights, smells, touch, people, other animals, situations and surfaces he or she is likely to encounter in his particular life. Consider your lifestyle and make a list of common activities your dog will encounter. Many lists will include "vacuum cleaner," "a visitor to our home," "grooming appointments" or "running children." One list may include "riding elevators," while someone else's list may include "horses and chickens." Perhaps a trip to a shopping center, playground, puppy playgroup, public library, or cafe would fit the bill. There is no way to introduce everything the puppy will need to feel at ease about. Rather, the idea is to at least come up with the most common things and provide happy exposure to those.

 You can have visitors take off their shoes before they enter as a precaution against disease. Although it's not necessary, if it will make it more likely you will give the pup a chance to learn about friends coming over, then shoes off it is! Train your pup right from the first visit alternatives to jumping up on guests with the tips in the Thank You for Not Jumping Up section of this book.

Don't Mess With Success (Why A Happy Exposure Is So Important)

Many people say they "mess with" the puppy while she is eating or "mess with" or touch her paws and tail to accustom her to that. This may work out, or what they may in fact be doing is teaching the puppy to find that kind of touch rather annoying (and then, paradoxically, they punish the puppy for becoming annoyed and reacting). If your goal is not mere tolerance of human touch, but rather you'd like to have a dog who actually wags her tail when you take a food item away or trim her nails, why not build in the right kind of association from the start? Teach the pup to happily accept human hands coming at her by pairing it with some of her meal. It can mean the difference between a big battle over these issues and helping the dog feel at ease. If you were the pup, which would you prefer?

Some people used to "alpha roll" puppies, supposedly to teach them who was "dominant." But like every field of knowledge, dog training and behavior has evolved. There are some approaches we continue with and some areas where we find a better, more up-to-date solution. Now we know that there is just no good reason to intimidate a dog in order to help him fit into your family or your life, or to show leadership (it turns out the alpha stuff is outdated advice based on misunderstandings about wolves). You certainly can use intimidation, and many people still do, but why go that route when there are kinder alternatives? It is much more respectful of the dog, allows kids to be part of the training, and allows you to avoid unintended fallout from using physical intimidation in the name of teaching.

It is easy to get started: just use this book and find a puppy class or dog trainer that uses modern, reward-based methods. You can still show leadership, create boundaries and meet expectations for good behavior. What have you got to lose by training in a way that works for both of you?

The Right Amount Of Happy Exposures

I recommend your puppy have a field trip, new visitor, or new item from your list at least five times per week. That factors in a couple of days when you may be extra busy and gives the puppy a chance to have some calmer days. An outing doesn't have to be longer than 5-10 minutes, and it's a lot less work than trying fix problems that otherwise might crop up later. An added bonus is that your puppy will likely behave like a dream the rest of the day because the excitement of something new tends to wear them out.

While a puppy class taught by an experienced instructor who advocates reward based methods certainly counts as a happy exposure, just be aware that by itself, attending puppy class does not mean you have socialized your puppy. Class is a great way for you to learn about appropriate greetings and play between puppies, house training, bite inhibition and basic training, and I highly recommend it. Going to the same class each week, with the same people and dogs, however, clearly only begins to help with your list. So, do attend class and then practice what you learned the rest of the week in novel surroundings with new people and dogs.

Remember, each puppy owner will have their own special list of socialization items depending on what they think life will have in store for their growing dog. Plan a happy new event at least five days a week. Make it fun by being encouraging, going at your puppy's pace, and pairing encounters with meals or a favorite toy. Enjoy your curious little fuzzball, because adolescence is not far behind!

Bold or Bashful?

Bold Puppy Tip: You may be tempted to rest on your laurels if your bold puppy swaggers through the world like everything is already familiar to him. Don't be fooled, don't be lazy, and don't leave him dangling when you should be telling him what a good sport he is when something wacky happens. It is also easy to let Mr. I'm Too Fabulous for Myself develop behaviors that seem playful now, but later will likely be interpreted as pushy or rude. So right off the bat (yes, starting at the age of 7 or 8 weeks old) be sure to elicit and reward behaviors you want to see in your pup as an adult: sitting before permission to approach someone rather than charging and leaping, encouraging putting his mouth on toys rather than on people's hands, getting treats while having his collar held by strangers rather than squirming and mouthing. Work on sharp responsiveness to his name starting now so you can redirect his attention to you no matter what else is going on. Then he really *will* be fabulous!

Bashful Puppy Tip: If new things, places, or sounds tend to elicit an especially hesitant reaction from your pup, teach a special happy game or two at home that you can take with you on the road. The key is to teach these games at home, in a safe space, so that your puppy loves them and can't wait to play them. Load the games with the highest value reward for your puppy (even if he could easily do them for just praise). The point is to create a portable oasis of safety and fun for encounters that occur beyond his comfort zone. It should only take a few training sessions to develop this association before you can use it out in the great, wide world.

Which games are best? For encountering objects or people your pup is not too sure about, a strong Nose Touch on cue will be a great asset. Cuing the puppy to Nose Touch a crazy-moving plastic bag, a new person's shoe, a giant garbage can in the neighborhood or the (at first turned off) vacuum cleaner can instantly put many puppies at ease. For sounds, movement or other intangibles, the Zippy Fast Recall game played according to the length of your leash can switch your puppy into a playful, easy-going mood and associate the new experience with feeling joyful. A game of tug can have the same effect, as can teaching a showy trick that involves a confident posture, like high five or spinning in each direction (playing dead in such a scenario does not really provide the emotional boost we're looking for, if you see what I mean). You'll be glad you have these upbeat games to play should you need them.

Chapter 17

Kids And Puppies

Ah, kids and puppies. On the TV commercials it always looks so blissful, puppies and little ones running around together in the grass, hard at work selling us toilet paper or diapers. Like most half-baked things we see on TV though, these scenes are a fantasy, as anyone who has tried to raise a puppy with kids can tell you. In real life, letting them run amok means inadvertently teaching your puppy to chase and nip the kids, and inadvertently teaching your kids to treat the puppy poorly in ways that could put them at risk down the line.

The kids need you to actively coach them on some rules. The puppy needs good habits instilled plus some daily downtime away from the kids. The first part of this section is about the rules, and the second part is about how to use the crate as a Safety Zone for your puppy's downtime. If you stick to those two things, you should be in good shape. For details on how to help your child and puppy become friends through the stages of your child's development, see *Happy Kids, Happy Dogs: Building a Friendship Right From the Start.*

Dos and Don'ts (For Kids and Adults)

First, the rules. Most parents teach their children important safety rules, such as: don't touch the electrical outlet, don't touch the stove, don't hit other children, look both ways before crossing the street and hold the scissors pointy end down. It takes effort to teach these, but it's worth it to prevent injury and mold a well-adjusted human. You wouldn't leave those things to chance.

Puppy-child interactions must also not be left to chance. Your child is depending on you to learn the correct way to be safe, kind and respectful from the very beginning. Not to mention that kids and their own or friends' dogs are in the highest risk category for dog bites. Other dogs are everywhere including at a friend's house, in the neighborhood, at an in-law's house, or at a soccer game. So the rules are not just about good manners and being respectful, they are about safety.

Children may (under adult supervision):

- Offer gentle, slow petting on the side of the puppy's face and under the chin

- Be a tree (still and quiet) rather than running and squealing in the puppy's presence

- Read to the puppy or listen to an adult read to both child and puppy

- Play Find It games (find your toy, the hidden treats, or a family member)

- Play the Animal Game (see the Jumping Up section)

- Help adult bake dog cookies

- Help adult groom the dog

- Help adult feed the dog

- Help adult fill the dog's water dish

- Feed treats while adult grooms the dog

- Help adult play fetch with the dog

- Help adult take the dog for walks (adult holds the leash)

- Sing quietly to the dog under adult supervision

- Count the dog's spots, feet, ears, tail, eyes, and legs under adult supervision

- Draw pictures of the dog

- Interact with, touch and greet dogs in the safe, correct way (see below)

- Help an adult teach or show off the dog's tricks (high five, spin, roll over, back up, take a bow, go night-night, nose touch, the list is endless!)

- Help an adult teach or show off the dog's cues (sit, down, come, etc.)

- Sit quietly on the floor with the pup only when the adult can see the pup is very sleepy and unlikely to be nippy (hold a giant plush dog toy just in case)

Adults must:

- Actively teach the kids what they can and should do, and reward them (this is different than supervision, which is passive and yields poor results with the combination of kids and dogs)

- Monitor the puppy for signs of stress (see below) or increasing arousal (leaping, zooming, biting)

- Use the Safety Zone before either the puppy or the kids start rehearsing the wrong behavior (see below)

- Be in charge of housetraining. Most kids under the age of 12 should not be in charge of housetraining; they can help at virtually any age by accompanying the adult, but they should not initiate potty breaks, crate use, or rewards and punishments. At best it will lengthen the process and at worst it could sabotage it. Housetraining is for grown-ups

- Tether the pup in the same room with an enticing food puzzle rather than letting him bother the kids while they eat meals, get ready for school, do their homework, or sit quietly to read or watch TV. This rewards the pup for lovely, calm behavior in the presence of the kids and helps them blend into each other's lives. (And it sure beats biting, crying, chasing, whining, barking and fighting. But maybe that's just me.)

- Block the puppy's view from running, screaming kids or confine him elsewhere with a chew toy. Tethering, chaining or fencing a dog in view of playing kids can lead to the rehearsal and build up of arousal and frustration in their presence, which can trigger chasing, leaping and biting. Kids should not be allowed to get in the habit of wild play, running and screaming in the presence of any dog.

- Never, ever leave the kids and dog unattended (especially infants, even if they are in a crib, car seat, or swing). It would probably turn out fine, but if it doesn't, it will turn badly too quickly for you to do a thing about it. Your puppy or dog should not be left to fend for himself. Your child should not be placed at risk when most dog bite injuries are preventable.

What might your child do to elicit a bite? Any of the following actions can easily threaten or frighten a dog. Do not allow your child to do any of these, whether on purpose or just absent-mindedly. In fact, don't do any of these things yourself, because they model the wrong behavior for your child and one day may put you or your child at risk with your dog or a friend's dog.

Hugging	Following the dog	Approaching a dog who is resting
Kissing	Chasing the dog	
Pinching	Touching from behind	Approaching a dog who is on his/her dog bed
Poking (nose, eyes, ears or anywhere else)	Using the dog to help stand up	
	Lying or standing on the dog	Approaching a dog who is sleeping
Wrestling		
Rough play, horse play	Leaning on the dog	Approaching a dog who is eating or chewing anything (if they are concerned, they should tell an adult, who should be right there with them anyway)
	Straddling the dog	
Running	Pulling or holding ears or tail	
Screaming		
Dressing the dog in outfits or hats	Grasping or pulling on the hair	
Lifting dog, partially or totally	Grabbing or touching paws	Approaching a dog who is chewing a toy or eating a meal
Carrying dog around	"Dancing" by holding	

Disturbing or interacting with a dog who is in a crate or otherwise confined (in a car, behind a baby gate, tethered with a chew toy, or tied outside a store or to a tree trunk)	paws Touching the dog with an object (like a doll, a stick, a spoon or a toy truck) Blowing air at the dog Playing outdoors or indoors with the dog without an adult present to coach them Approaching a dog who is in his Safety Zone	Throwing things at the dog, or in the direction of the dog Hitting or kicking the dog, either slightly or roughly, or touching the dog with a foot Anything that elicits dog warning signs (see below)

If you think your dog is fine with any of the items above, you probably have not noticed signs of stress that are subtler than biting or growling, but which are clear signs of stress. They include:

- Turning the head away

- Walking away

- Yawning

- Lip licking

- Shaking off as though wet

- Shallow panting

- Scratching

- Stretching

- Stiffening or freezing

- Whites of eyes flashing, furtive glancing

By now you may be thinking this is a lot of fuss over nothing. Ask yourself this: How many times would you tolerate inappropriate touch from someone? If they kept touching you inappropriately, how would you respond? It is risky and just plain unfair to expect a dog to tolerate these things over and over. One mother asked me why it wasn't ok to let her 7 year old son endlessly follow their dog around, holding him by the tail, while the dog continued to try to get away (with his head lowered, ears back and brow furrowed). Please put yourself in your puppy's position and encourage your kids to do the same. It is an important lesson that will serve them their whole lives every time they interact with others.

Even if your dog truly loves everything on the Don'ts list (which he probably doesn't, not if you really ask him by monitoring his stress signals), you are setting your child up for a bite by another dog if you allow rehearsal of the Don'ts at home with your dog. A tolerant dog and a fearless child are a recipe for disrespect at best, and injury at worst. Isn't now the perfect time to start teaching your child to take your dog's feelings into account?

The Safety Zone

Every dog, no matter how docile, needs an indoor spot that will allow him to relax undisturbed by children. Every child, no matter how at ease around dogs, needs to learn to respect their space. When a dog is in his Safety Zone, children may not look at or interact with him. Using the Safety Zone correctly means greater safety for your child and his playmates, and more peace for everyone when it's time for a break.

Step One

Where to set up the Safety Zone

Choose a room to confine your pup such that he can still smell and hear many household activities, but without being in the thick of things. Provide fresh water, meals, edible toys and comfy bedding for your dog in the Safety Zone. The Safety Zone can just be your puppy's crate. Once your puppy is house-trained, consider using a larger crate as the Safety Zone for extra space and comfort. You can also baby gate a room you don't use very much. This option allows you to confine your dog to a low-traffic room adjacent to family activity, like the dining room. Nowadays gates come in all heights and lengths. You could also use an exercise pen ('x-pen' for short). It has panels so that you can fold it up to carry or store.

Step Two

When to introduce and use the Safety Zone

If you don't yet have kids but you're expecting a baby, start using the Safety Zone a few times daily no later than four weeks before the baby's arrival. If you already have kids, or if kids visit your home, introduce the Safety Zone now.

Despite what you may have heard, supervision does not prevent dog bites to children. You must be a kid canine coach, which means you actively promote and reward good behavior by your child and your dog. Any time you cannot coach your dog and child through their interactions, use the Safety Zone. Examples:

- It's the morning rush and you are multi-tasking like bananas

- Company comes over and things are a bit exciting

- You are too busy or too tired to be an effective coach

- Your child's playmates are visiting and you need a break from coaching all of them

- You have a babysitter or housekeeper over

- Front-door traffic might pose an opportunity for doggie escape

Even after your puppy is housetrained and has learned to chew only on his things, use a version of the Safety Zone, like a baby gated room or x-pen, when you can't coach your children and puppy.

As long as you continue to meet your puppy's daily needs for aerobic exercise, affection, and training, there is no need to feel guilty about using the Safety Zone. It provides an important break for your growing dog and keeps your kids from experimenting with your dog.

Chapter 18

Peaceful Pets

Here are the guidelines for helping your puppy become a beloved member of the family, rather than a huge brat that causes stress for your other dog or cat.

Manage Introductions

To introduce your pup to your other dog, arrange to have a helper meet you in a neutral location (like a parking lot near your house) with your resident dog. But don't let them approach each other at first. Instead, take a 3-5 minute walk around the area, with your current resident dog out in front with your helper, and you and the new puppy following about 20 feet behind. Gradually let the pup catch up, until the two dogs are strolling along, parallel with each other but at least five feet apart. One or the other (or both) may lean in for a sniff of the other, which is perfectly okay. However, don't stop if this happens; just keep walking regardless, so that the puppy doesn't jump up and so the resident dog doesn't get bombarded or overreact.

If possible, walk home together from this neutral location (or drive them home separately) and explore the yard in the same way. Then go indoors, resident dog first, and do the same thing throughout the house. Then baby gate the puppy in his confinement area so the other dog gets a break and the puppy can nap after all that excitement.

Introduce Valued Objects Gradually

Start off with no toys, bedding or bowls that could be claimed by one dog or the other (dole them out and pick them up selectively, using gates or crates to separate the dogs during use). As it's clear the dogs are getting along, gradually add an item or two over a few days provided they continue to remain nonchalant about the other dog passing by when they are engaged with the valued item.

Create Boundaries Before Trouble Starts

From the first day forward, your puppy should engage with your other dog when you decide you are in the mood to supervise a play session. Interactions between your puppy and other pets should begin because you decide it's time, not because the puppy wants to pounce on everyone.

Several five-minute sessions a day are plenty until you get into a rhythm with your pup and it's clear your other pets feel relaxed in his presence. Start outdoors (in a safe, fenced area) where there's likely to be more space for all the doggie body language communication they need. A large room with good traction underfoot works well, too.

Start by letting your older dog out first. Then, with your pup on a leash, make a couple of loops together around the yard and then casually let the puppy's leash drop while you keep walking. Your puppy will likely approach your other dog right away, possibly leaping at the older dog's face or play bowing. Most mature dogs are patient with puppies, and are also good at giving a quick freeze-in-place or mild growl if the pup is going a little too bonkers. This is very good for the puppy, because it is normal dog communication that he needs to become skilled at recognizing and using. They may or not play, and as long as they keep moving (because you keep walking), it will probably go smoothly. You can always pick up the pup's leash if you are not sure about an interaction, and quietly step between the two if you need them to separate.

How To Help An Older Dog, Or, "Mom, Why Have You Ruined My Life By Bringing Home This Horrible Creature?"

Your mature dog may occasionally communicate to your pup that he needs to tone his antics down a notch, which is perfectly okay (you may see your older dog exhibit freezing in place with a sidelong glance, a growl, a snap, or even a quick lunge or gentle nose grab). It is usually only a problem if the pup does not tone down his enthusiasm in response to the older dog's signals to simmer down. If your older dog has to remind him a second time, it's best to silently and calmly remove the pup (by guiding him by his drag line, picking him up, or distracting him with a treat) and letting him chill out in his own space. If you don't intervene, a) your puppy may learn it's fun to be out of control, setting him up for failure with other dogs and/or b) your older dog may learn to start bringing out the big guns, which may scare the living daylights out of your puppy. Again, most puppies and dogs work this out well if you set them up for success by planning sessions, keeping them short, and intervening before anyone gets too bratty or impatient.

If your other dog shows no interest in your puppy, by all means do not allow your puppy to pester him with abandon. For now, keep them separated with a gate or exercise pen. Or, use a very lightweight drag line with the puppy that you can step on to restrict his movement toward the other dog as needed.

Reward your older dog with low-key praise and attention (like some loving eye contact) whenever the pup enters the room, passes near him, or approaches you, so that he will associate the puppy's presence with extra good feelings. When both dogs approach you at the same time, keep your emotions low-key at first, greeting the pup briefly and then greeting the older dog. Greet the pup first not because the puppy is better or cuter, but rather to teach the older dog that when the little whippersnapper gets attention, it predicts even more attention for the mature dog. If either of the dogs cuts each other off or tries to shove their way towards you, simply walk away. They will learn that shoving for attention causes withdrawal of your attention, the opposite of their intention.

If you have any concerns that your older dog may be getting quite jealous or protective of you, walk away by stepping toward and between the dogs, and then separate them for a break. Ideally you will teach your pup to sit on cue within a couple of days, so that any time they are near you, they will both be inclined to sit automatically in exchange for treats and attention. (However if you have concerns about food guarding by either of them check with a qualified trainer on how to best handle this exercise.) It can be helpful to release your puppy from the sit before releasing your adult dog, so that he's inclined to follow you as you walk away and not pounce on his buddy. (Phew, puppies are exhausting; there is so much to think about. I got tired just writing that paragraph!)

Go on walks together, so they can learn to hang out in a way that does not involve the pup learning to annoy your other dog.

Keep up your other dog's exercise routines, and consider throwing in some micro training every day by having him do a sit or other trick in exchange for things he wants. Both of these will add some structure and predictability to his life in the midst of such a big change. If he tends to be the worrying type, consider getting him a CEVA brand Adaptil collar to ease the transition.

Observe how the dogs are doing when valued objects like a toy or chew bone are added into their environment. It is normal for dogs to be protective of objects or food in their possession. A briefly frozen body posture, "stink" eye (a hard, oblique stare), or even a growl are usually not cause for concern when displayed toward another dog and when that communication does not cause an escalation in the interaction between them. However, if your dog seems aggressive towards (for example lunging toward or not relenting when the pup retreats after subtler signals are given) or fearful of your puppy, or if your dog has had trouble in the past with aggression over valued items, consult a dog trainer for advice on the safest and most productive way to proceed.

The Cat's Meow

However amusing it may seem, it is not a good idea to let your puppy rehearse chasing or poking your kitty. It's not fair to either of them, and one of them could be injured. Don't wing it. Use these strategies until they are at ease around each other:

- Let your pup drag a long line so you can step on it quickly in case he gets the urge to chase the kitty. (Provide your puppy with appropriate chase outlets like fetch and chasing you in come-when-called games.)

- Keep a handful of treats in your pocket and each time your puppy's attention turns to your cat, say "good!" and pop a treat in his mouth. At worst you may put some treats through the wash at the end of the day. At best, your puppy will figure out that the appearance of the cat predicts getting a goodie from you, rather than the start of a chase game. I know what you're thinking, but you are not teaching the pup to look at the cat. You are creating an emotional association that results in the pup spotting the cat and then whipping his head toward you in anticipation of a treat.

- Regardless of your puppy's intentions with the cat, if you prevent chasing with a drag line and you are consistent with the treats, soon (usually in just a few days) your pup will see the cat and this will prompt him to look at you. Cool!

- Give your pup a chance to get used to your cat and visa versa by letting them interact with a baby gate or exercise pen between them.

- Make sure your cat has escape routes (like the ability to jump over, or scamper under, a baby gate).

- Consider keeping the cat's food up high so he can eat in peace.

- Keep the litter box in a space that only the cat can reach, or the puppy will find a special snack there and you will never, ever want him to lick your face again.

- If your cat is one of those precocious types who tries to entice your puppy by strutting right under his nose to get something started, at least get it on video so the rest of us can enjoy it. Meanwhile just keep up your puppy's training and be glad your cat is not afraid of him.

Chapter 19

Car Rides

Cure Carsickness

During or after a car ride your puppy may show signs of carsickness. He may tremble, salivate, and/or vomit. While carsickness is common in puppies, if you merely wait for your puppy to outgrow it he could associate the car with the unpleasant feeling of motion sickness, and get in the habit of feeling nervous about getting into the car. That feeling of dread leads to queasiness, which in turn perpetuates the problem of getting sick in the car. Gack! You can further contribute to your pup's fear of the car by taking him only to places that he associates mainly with stress, like to veterinary or grooming appointments or to be boarded. Double gack!

What to do? It makes no sense to punish your puppy for getting sick in the car (if you got car sick would it help you get over it if someone scolded you?). It might even make it worse, since your pup would have something additional to fear (your reactions) related to the car.

Instead, the following strategies should put your puppy on the road to enjoying car trips. By doing them all (which I recommend), you will likely find he will be over his problem in a week or two. Not bad, huh?

- Set up a crate for your dog to ride in. Cover it with a sheet so that he can't see the world zipping and bouncing past him. Make sure there is airflow along the bottom third of the crate so fresh air reaches him.

- Secure the crate so it is stable. It should not tip or slide (use bungee cords out of reach of little teeth, and/or a folded blanket underneath the crate to make it level).

- 15 minutes before each car trip: a) feed your pooch a couple of ginger snaps, which can help calm the tummy, and b) spray the crate bedding with calming dog appeasing pheromone (the CEVA brand Adaptil spray is best). Limit bedding to an easily washed, old towel at this point.

- Start with very short trips. Drive no more than 1/2 a block, then gently take your puppy out of the car and do something he loves, like take a walk or play a game of tug. Then drive the short distance back home. These mini trips are short enough to prevent tummy upset and long enough to be the tip-off for a really fun activity.

- Extend the distance you drive one block at a time, as long as your pup does not get sick, is relaxed and drool-free.

This series of "fake," short trips that reliably predict a happy event should lead to a pretty quick and permanent fix.

Once your puppy is confident and relaxed in the car, if you prefer not to use a crate for car rides, use a doggie seat belt for everyone's safety and to instill good car-riding habits. Either way, a nice edible chew toy or peanut butter Kong on a towel are a great way to keep the puppy from developing bad habits like barking out the window, whining, or chewing on the seatbelts.

Bold or Bashful?

Bold Puppy Tip: Beware of the little rascal trying to launch himself into, and especially out of, the car before and after trips. He could injure himself more easily than you can imagine, and then develop reluctance to get in the car to boot. I know he's a baby but teach him good habits right away; he should sit patiently, even after you open the car door, for permission to hop in or out. (And of course as a puppy he shouldn't be hopping in and out at all, just lift him into your arms so you can safely put him in or take him out of the car.) Think twice about letting him ride with his head out the window, or at least get him a pair of doggie goggles to protect his eyes from airborne debris. I am sure he can pull off that look.

Bashful Puppy Tip: You might be tempted to let the pup ride in your lap or on the seat beside you. I know, I know, he is very fluffy and sweet and just wants to curl up in your lap. But here's the thing. Besides being unsafe (for you and other motorists due to how distracting it is, and for the puppy in the event you hit the brakes), you are setting up for a difficult transition that the poor dude won't even see coming. Sometime soon the puppy is going to be too large to sit in your lap, and you are going to have to break it to him that he has to sit all by himself, where he can't even see you. Holy Doggie Drama, Batman, the wailing that will ensue! Avoid all that by snuggling with the pup at home on the family room floor (he will make it easier to get through the awful evening news), and letting him ride in the car just like he will as an adult.

 It can be dangerous (and in many places illegal) to leave a puppy or dog in a car when it is 70 degrees outside or warmer. Even with windows cracked, doing so can mean brain damage for your dog in the minutes it takes you to run an errand. In ten minutes your car can reach 102 degrees, and organ damage can begin when your dog's body temperature reaches 107 degrees. Think about the greenhouse effect created by the enclosed car plus the dog exhaling air that is 100% humid as he pants to stay cool. Please do not leave your puppy in the car when it is 70 degrees or warmer, okay?

Part IV
Training Skills To Better Communicate With Your Puppy

Chapter 20

Ten Secrets Of The Pros To Make Your Training Fast And Effective

You'll be tempted to grab some treats and jump into your training, but you may be disappointed in the results if you don't follow these tried and true guidelines to set yourselves up for success.

1. Start all training in a distraction-free environment. This could be a bathroom, a gated hallway, a mudroom, or anywhere that you are the most interesting thing to your puppy just by standing there.

2. Keep training sessions under five minutes in length. It is okay to train several five-minute sessions a day.

3. Sandwich your training between two bouts of play. Start and end each training session with 30 seconds of running around, tug or fetch. This keeps your pup lively, interested and sharp. It also teaches him how to switch from feeling wild to being calm. Most importantly, it instills in him a love for play and training with you, which over time means great results any time, anywhere.

4. Always be generous with your praise and rewards. If you aren't feeling generous and happy, your training session will suffer. We're only human; just try again later.

5. Cut up all your treats ahead of time so there is no fumbling around on your part. Fumbles mean delays, which confuse your pup because precious reward opportunities are lost (when this happens there is a ripple in the universe that all dog trainers feel).

6. Treats or kibble should be no larger than a pea so they require no chewing. Minimize distracting crumbs by choosing small or soft treats (like macaroni cooked in broth or Buddy Biscuit soft treats).

7. Train when your puppy is fully awake, has recently pottied and has an appetite.

8. When an exercise seems easy, it is very important to move on to the next level of difficulty to avoid getting stuck. As soon as your pup catches on, add one distraction at a time. This could be moving to a different room, going outside, having others nearby, trying it at the park, or by adding duration or several quick repetitions before rewarding.

9. If your puppy doesn't do what you had hoped, he is not giving you the bird, I promise. He is giving you precious information that it is time to trouble-shoot what you are doing. Are you following the directions exactly? Are your rewards truly rewarding according to your puppy? Are you in a slightly too-distracting environment? Are you feeling frustrated or impatient? Does he need to be energized with a game first? Does your pup need a physical need met before he can concentrate? Does he feel safe? All of these factors can play a role in your puppy's ability to succeed at what you're trying to teach. In other words, it's not him, it's you. Yes, dog training is the world's most humbling activity. We have all been there. Just know you will be proud as a peacock when it all comes together!

10. Take a minute of video so if you really get stuck you can easily get help. Seriously, upload it to YouTube and I will help you.

Chapter 21

Teach Your Puppy Her New Name

This is a fun, easy and important step in bonding with and communicating with your pup. The key to teaching your pup her new name is to create an incredibly pleasant association between the sound of the new name and your pup's attention to you. Here's how.

You will need about 90 seconds out of your day, ten scrumptious treats, and a distraction-free, indoor room.

Let's say you've decided to name your puppy "Fifi." (Please don't actually do that, it's just an example.)

Step One

Stand no further than one foot away from her in a quiet, indoor space. In a cheerful, normal-volume voice, say, "Fifi!" once only.

Step Two

If she turns toward you, or even just flicks an ear toward you, instantly identify that response by saying "good!" and feed one treat.

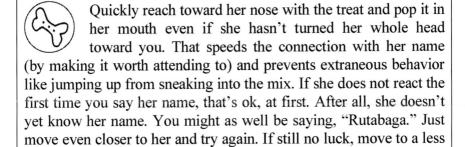 Quickly reach toward her nose with the treat and pop it in her mouth even if she hasn't turned her whole head toward you. That speeds the connection with her name (by making it worth attending to) and prevents extraneous behavior like jumping up from sneaking into the mix. If she does not react the first time you say her name, that's ok, at first. After all, she doesn't yet know her name. You might as well be saying, "Rutabaga." Just move even closer to her and try again. If still no luck, move to a less distracting environment, like a small powder room, and try again.

Step Three

Do that nine more times. "Fifi!" (she looks) "Good!" (you feed a treat). Repeat. If she keeps looking at you between repetitions, feed a treat anyway.

Practice 3-5 times a day.

When that's easy (likely after a session or two), increase your distance from her by a few feet (no more than that, or you will be hurrying toward failure).

Still easy? Here is a bonus. Extend the concept of name recognition to mean sticking to you when she hears her name, like so:

Step One

Say her name once. When she looks your way, say "good" and run the other way! (Please look where you're going or you might end up with a black eye.)

Step Two

When she catches up, feed many pieces of food, but feed them one at a time. Do this like you are a game show host doling out $20 bills, one after another, for dramatic effect. Feed close to your body (that prevents 'fly-by's') and hold your hands low (that prevents jumping up). You will not be able to resist praising her lavishly, because you'll be so excited to see what a genius she is, so I don't think I even need to mention that part.

To advance her training, master the above exercise in each of the following locations (outdoors, use a fence or a leash):

- Indoors, all rooms (use familiar rooms first, then less familiar rooms)
- Indoors with distraction (like a person walking by or animal noises on TV)
- Outdoors in low distraction areas (perhaps a patio)
- Outdoors in more challenging areas (perhaps in front of the house)

- Outdoors with mild distractions (perhaps a toy lying still, then a toy moving)

- Outdoors with more challenging distractions (like a bird nearby or a person approaching)

"Voila!" says Fifi in her French accent, "Now I know my name!"

Bold or Bashful?

Bold Puppy Tip: Consider feeding some of your pup's meals by hand in place of treats for these exercises. It will create an even stronger, more positive association with her name since it is being paired with her basic nutritional needs. This will translate to a stronger foundation of good responses before you venture into more distracting locations. By building your pup's reflex to respond, you make it less tempting to leave you for other adventures.

Bashful Puppy Tip: Beware of using lots of patting and reaching for your bashful pup; it is much better simply to hold the treats close to your body and feed them while praising. Many a person has inadvertently taught their pup to stay just out of arm's length to avoid the mild unpleasantness of reaching, looming and head patting that we humans can't seem to get enough of. Build your pup's confidence by pairing rewards with the act of coming close enough to you to touch.

Chapter 22

The Nose Touch: The Best Kept Secret In Dog Training

This simple behavior is a whole bag of useful tricks rolled into one. It will solve myriad issues, literally with the wave of a hand. Teach this to your puppy and you'll wonder how you would have gotten along without it.

The goal: after a few short training sessions you will be able to say, "Touch!" and your pup will swiftly bop the palm of your hand with the tip of his nose.

Why in the world would you teach that? The nose touch will make your life easier and helps bold as well as bashful puppies because it:

- Helps your puppy to learn to touch your hands with a closed mouth (self control instead of biting teeth)

- Teaches your puppy to feel happy about people's hands near his face, which is important for grooming, veterinary visits, meeting new people and interactions with children

- Transfers to other objects, so you can ask your pup to nose touch people's hands or shoes instead of leaping on them in greeting

- Helps a puppy feel confident about unfamiliar objects (like a vacuum cleaner, wheel barrow or stethoscope) because the interaction becomes a nose touch game rather than a "yikes, what the heck is that thing!?" encounter

- Allows you to position your puppy any way you want (beside you on a leash walk, away from a toddler if they get in a tight space together, lined up for the veterinary examination, for a photo, or to teach a trick like "twirl in a circle," "sit pretty" or "roll over")

- Gives your child and puppy a great game to play together that involves self control on both their parts

- Gives your pup something fun to do when he might be nervous (like in the waiting room at the veterinarian's office, waiting his turn in group training class, or in between ears when you're cleaning them)

- Refocuses your dog on you just *before* he has the chance to stare at another dog, a cat, or something else that you've spotted ahead of time that is none of his beeswax. (Don't wait until he's already staring to cue the nose touch, because it probably won't work at this stage and it might even link up the two actions in a way you hadn't intended.)

Session One (5 minutes)

For your first session, keep one hand clean and keep three treats in the other. The clean hand is the hand your dog will touch with his nose. Use tiny, non-crumbly treats. Crumbs may cause you to say bad words when they distract your pup. Bend at the waist or sit in a chair or on the floor, whatever is most comfortable.

Step One

Hide your clean "touch" hand behind your back. This will pique your pup's interest. Your pup may nuzzle the other hand holding the treats. Just ignore that and make a fist around the treats (don't hide the treat hand or pull it out of his reach). Keep the treat hand motionless or it will become very fascinating. Just stay still and ignore the nuzzling.

Step Two

Present your rigidly flat palm roughly nose-level with your pup, about a foot away from him. Say nothing. Just wait. Make sure your thumb is parallel to the ceiling. Be ready! Many dogs will immediately bop your palm (or at least sniff it) the first few attempts. This is sheer luck, but you still want to be ready to reward.

Step Three

The instant he bumps your hand with his nose, or even comes close at first (don't be greedy), keep your touch hand right where it is as you say "yes!" and deliver a treat with your other, treat hand. Ideally, reach over and place the treat as close as possible to the spot where your dog bopped your palm and let your dog take the treat at the spot.
    Repeat 5-6 times in a row.

 If you get any biting, hide your hand behind your back and on the next repetition, hold your hand closer to your pup and reward just for your pup's mouth being closed, even if he makes no contact with your hand at first. If the little dude is really feisty, find a calmer time of day to begin this training, and tether him to the coffee table to give him fewer wild-man options during training.

If your puppy gets stuck:

- Look at your touch hand, not the dog
- Hide your hand and then make it reappear ("flash" it); works for most puppies
- Just be patient and let them puzzle it out
- Reward "almost" touching just once to help jump-start the process
- If your pup gets stuck in a sit (standing is much preferred), toss a treat slightly away from you to help "reset" them

Congratulations! You've completed your first touch training session.

Session Two

(5 minutes; this could be after you have a little party, running around in celebration of Session One, or later the same day)

Step One

Repeat as above. When it's going well and you've had three solid nose touches followed by treats, pause after the next touch rather than rewarding. 99.9% of puppies will think, "Hey, lady! Where's my cookie, did you not see that I did a nose touch?" and they will try again. Reward and praise heartily.

Step Two

Now flash your hand, your pup should touch it, then move it to another position (still at nose-level) one direction or another. Reward near your nose touch hand.

Step Three

Time to switch hands! Your other hand is now the clean, nose touch hand and you will deliver treats with the opposite hand. Fancy!

Session Three

(5 minutes; wait a few hours at least before session three for best results)

You may now add your cue word, since it will become the cue for the polished action that you really like. If you don't have that polished action yet, practice a few more sessions first.

Choose one word and stick to it. You might like "Touch!" or "Bop it!" or "Nosey!" The key is to say the word, pause a beat, and only then present your flat palm as usual.

You now have a puppy who will touch the tip of her nose to your hand. To make it practical for real life, add distractions gradually. Try it outside (use even better treats) and get other family members, your veterinarian, and friends in on the game. Explain it, demonstrate for them, then let them try.

To transfer it to an object, hold a plastic lid near your palm, give your cue, hold out the lid, and reward like bananas. What a genius your puppy is! Put the lid in different spots. Then replace the lid with other objects your dog feels fine about, so he is the nose touch master (it helps to cue touching the lid, then the new object, then the lid to help generalize the concept).

At that stage you can use the nose touch to help him adjust to an object that unnerves him. Turning something into a nose touch game is often all it takes to overcome a low-level fear. You can have him touch the toenail file, instruments at the veterinary office, grooming tools, the ear drop bottle, or his harness. Continue to reward generously and pretty soon the nose touch will be rewarding in itself.

Bold or Bashful?

Bold Puppy Tip: During initial training your little whippersnapper may try to bite your hand rather than bop it with his nose. If you see his jaws parting on approach, swiftly withdraw your hand and hold it behind your back for a moment. This works in one or two repetitions. If it doesn't, you need to choose a less-stimulating time of day or less interesting treats to help tone things down. The nose touch will be a terrific skill to prevent crotch sniffing, pulling on leash and other bold puppy tendencies, so it's worth the small effort to teach.

Bashful Puppy Tip: This is so important for your bashful pup that you should teach it right along with potty training and his name. As soon as he is very proud of himself during this game, have him do it with all family members, then friends, neighbors, and finally strangers. Break out the best treats and make it one of his favorite tricks. It will make exploring the world, being examined and greeted by others, and getting in the car (as he aims for the lid) a snap!

Chapter 23

Sit On Cue

According to everyone, you should teach your puppy to sit. This may be mind-blowing, but your puppy already knows how to sit. He doesn't need any help from you to learn that. The useful part is for your puppy to learn to sit reliably on your cue. Or, in response to convenient environmental cues like your hand reaching for a doorknob, the appearance of a supper bowl, the leash in your hand, a guest saying hello, or some food accidentally dropped on the floor. This keeps your puppy safe, out of trouble, attentive to you, and from scratching anyone's legs by jumping up.

Could you instead teach your pup to freeze in a standing position with all four paws on the floor for the same effect? Sure. But sit on cue is nice because all that puppy weight sinks down into his little caboose and helps him stay put. It is also easier for humans to evaluate whether a puppy is sitting still (versus standing still), so the training goes more smoothly. Sit-on-cue is also a great option for bold puppies who may need something constructive to do with their brain and body, and for bashful puppies because it builds confidence (provided you train it with kindness).

Okay, so we've established your pup already knows how to sit. We just need to help him be aware of that bodily action and then show him it is in his best interests to offer it a lot. We will also let him know when it's ok to pop out of the sit position. Finally, we will add the cherry on top of getting him to offer sit on cue or even automatically, when a little self-control is helpful for everyone involved.

Dear Puppy, Did You Know Sitting Pays Big Dividends?

Carry a pocket full of kibble or special treats around for a day or two, and every time your pup happens to sit on his own, instantly say "good!" and pop a piece of kibble in his mouth. Lickity split he will figure out that something marvelous happens to him every time he plants his hiney on the floor! Maybe he'll sit only twice the first day. Not to worry, soon this number will increase exponentially if you are quick to say, "good!" and reward.

When you deliver the treat, think of how your puppy's behind will stay planted better if you deliver the treat from above his head, like how a mamma bird feeds a baby bird.

Perhaps you're thinking, "Don't I have to say 'sit'?" Here's another mind-blowing puppy training fact: the word "sit" does not motivate your puppy to sit. He has no idea what that word means. Most humans are very invested in our fancy verbal-ness. However, what motivates your puppy to sit often (and to stay there) is how rewarding you make it after he does it.

Yes, you read right. It's what comes after the sit that makes him want to do it more often, better, quicker and longer. So for now focus on your reward delivery after he sits, and soon you'll get to introduce the verbal cue.

When your pup is barely finished swallowing his goodie, cheerfully say, "ok" and pat your leg, walking away so it is loud and clear you are encouraging him to get up from the sit position. You might as well introduce that "permission to get up" concept right off the bat, since sit is useless if our dogs sit on cue, but then instantly get up and bolt away.

So far it looks like this:

> You carry treats in your pocket
> Your pup just happens to sit
> You see it and say "good!"
> You promptly pop a treat in his mouth, baby-bird style while he's sitting
> You say "ok" to encourage him to walk out of the sit position

Dear Puppy, Did You Know That There Are Things That Can Tip You Off That Sitting Would Pay Off Big If You Did It Right This Second?

Barbara Shumannfang   151

After two or three days (no kidding, it's fast!) your puppy will start sitting quite frequently in hopes of being paid with a goodie. Which of course you will provide. This is just right for the first stage. (And may I say, good job.)

If you'd like to have a human word that cues the sit (I highly recommend it), just say "sit" (meaningless at first). Then wait (be patient, he will sit only because it's been paying big dividends lately). Then say "good!" and deliver his treat, and finally release him from position with "ok."

It could take just a few to up to several dozen repetitions before your pup has learned that the human word sit is the tip-off to get his butt into that position. (Imagine if you were learning a foreign language that at first you didn't even realize was a language. Try to be patient.) Say the word just one to two seconds before he starts to do the action and that will help. Now you can start using his new word around the house and outside, rewarding with extra special goodies for sitting on cue in these new surroundings. He is a genius! Remember to say "ok" after he swallows the treat so he knows it's time to get up.

Now, choose something with very black-and-white boundaries, like whether his suppertime food puzzle touches the floor or not. Or whether you open the door to the backyard or not, or the door to his crate to let him out or not. (Save leash on or not, onto furniture or not, or getting petted or not for next week. They can be a little squishier to manage. Get these basics solid first.)

Let's pick offering him his meal in a food puzzle. Hold it and wait, silently. Don't do anything bossy like pushing your puppy's butt to the ground or leaning over to intimidate him into sitting (boo-hiss!). Just wait. (Ignore whining, leaping, anything that isn't sitting. He's not naughty, he's just trying to figure out what works quickest to get the payoff. If you respond, he may perceive it as a reward, and rewards are very powerful for building behavior, including behavior you don't like!)

Be ready, because your puppy knows full well what pays big-time. His puppy wheels will turn and he will sit. You don't believe me, I know you don't, but that's okay because when he sits you will think, "I have the world's smartest puppy!!!" Try to stay focused and say, "good!" as usual, and present the food puzzle. Then you can do your happy dance.

To keep things extra clear for him and for you, as you're reaching for the floor to place the food puzzle down, say "ok!" to signal it's ok to get up from the sit to get the toy.

After a couple of days, you holding his supper will become a cue to offer the sit position. Think about what other, everyday situations it would be handy to have your puppy recognize as cues to automatically sit and hold still until released. You can teach those, too, the sky's the limit!

Puppy Sit On Cue FAQ's

"Can't I just get him to follow a treat or toy that I hold overhead until he sits, and then reward him?"

Sure. Just know that it is bribery. Bribery only gets you so far. Your puppy will quickly start assessing the quality of the food or toy and comparing it to what other interesting stuff the universe has to offer. Then he might do the sit, or opt for something more interesting (who could blame him?). This is the "he'll only do it if I have a treat syndrome." Ack! Personally, I prefer that the puppy choose to sit of his own volition, with purpose and clarity from the get-go (rather than weighing his options) since I want that kind of strong commitment associated with my verbal cue. That is the kind of training that holds up when I have company over.

"But in puppy class they recommend we lure with a treat, will it mess things up if I try it?"

If you decide to lure him into a sit position, I'd recommend doing so no more than two times and then proceeding as above. Some people say it's faster to start by luring; if you need your puppy to offer sits like crazy by the end of day one because he just landed a Cottonelle TV commercial and you have no time to lose, then by all means go for it! This also goes for puppies in a shelter, whose lives may depend on how quickly they can learn to impress potential adopters they can sit when prompted. Be aware if you lure more than a few times you will need to gradually fade your arm movement (or turn it into a cue) as well as fade the bribery out of the picture.

"My puppy is built like a coffee table. I promise I've been watching for it, but I never see him just sit on his own. What should I do?"

If he prefers to lie down, you could teach him a cue for lying down using the same approach. Or watch like a hawk; most puppies sit on their way into the down position. Watch for that at times he is sleepy or headed over to spots he likes to lie, and start saying, "good!" for that nanosecond-long sit. Please enjoy the look of surprise on his face when he figures out his butt can do that and it pays to do so. And be extra particular about feeding him from up high like he's a baby bird to help emphasize the lowering of the butt while keeping the head up is the key.

"Sit is going great, but how do I teach him to stay?"

You have already started! By remembering to clearly release him from position by saying "ok" after each time he gets rewarded for a sit, you have been doing mini-stays. (Surprise!) To draw out the length of time he holds the sit-stay, simply withhold the treat for one second, then feed, then release with "ok." It looks like so:

> Puppy sits (your word or the environment cues)
> You say "good!"
> You count in your head "one-banana"
> You feed the goodie, baby bird style
> You release with "ok"

Dog trainers have whole conferences on whether you should add on to the duration of the sit-stay in consecutive seconds, or whether it's best to hop from one second, to three seconds, back to two, up to five and so on (rewarding for each duration in either case). Heck, just do what makes sense to you and does not tempt your puppy to get up. If he gets up, it means you waited too long before rewarding. It is information for you that 4 seconds was too advanced and he needs more time with 1, 2 and 3-second stays. (Or your rewards are ho-hum, or the environment is too distracting. You get the picture; the dog never lies.) Once he gets it, ka-pow, you will be able to progress to a one-minute stay within a couple of weeks. Really! (Oh, and please do not call your puppy to you from the sit stay and reward him with the treat. That is rewarding him for moving out of position, and for the sit-stay we want to make the staying put part rewarding. Feed his reward while he's in the stay position. You can get fancy with mixing your training cues up once the basics are solid a few months from now.)

"That's the problem; I can't get him to move out of the sit, no matter how cheerfully I say 'ok.'"

Isn't that a great problem? You have taught your puppy that it is so rewarding to sit on cue that you can't get him to move! If he gets stuck do not repeat the release word, coax him or do cartwheels. Just walk straight towards and barely past him as you say "ok," which will throw him a little off-center as he looks to see where you're going, and when he gets up out of the sit position, praise and feed him a treat for coming up to you. Occasionally throw one of those moving-toward-him releases in and reward it, and once he gets the hang of hopping up on "ok," reward him for getting up every 5th sit or so.

"I think my puppy is made of pudding; as soon as he sits, even if I say "good!" he just flops into a down position. It's as though he has no bones. Does he need to see an orthopedist?"

Geez, puppies are cute. (Someone had to say it.) For puppies like this, the key is in how you deliver the reward. You have to be lightening quick, not only with your reward word but also with swooping in with the reward, and you absolutely must feed from very high over his head. Pretend you are a giant crane delivering the goodie from straight above. In cases of extreme floppiness, you can even say "good!" when he's roughly in a sit and then instantly throw the treat slightly behind him for him to chase after (just do that a few times, until he forgets all about the lying down part). Meanwhile choose your practice location carefully; a surface with good traction, like carpet, is better so he won't be inclined to slide onto the floor.

Chapter 24

Thank You For Not Jumping Up

Dogs jump up on people in greeting, out of excitement, or to get our attention. However, most people don't like it and wish their puppy wouldn't start that habit. If your puppy jumps up, and you respond by pushing your pup away or speaking to him (even if you're saying "no!" "down" or "off"), you are rewarding the jumping up with touch and attention. When dogs are rewarded for doing something over and over, they get very good at it. Thus, a cycle of jumping up is created. Not to mention, I get to use the word "thus."

Fortunately there is a way out of this cycle. The following plan will help you drastically reduce, if not eliminate, jumping up. It works because it is based on how dogs learn: it strategically uses what they want as a reward for the kind of behavior we want. Be consistent. Everyone in the family must follow the plan. Jumping up can be a thing of the past within two to three weeks if you stick to this plan like glue.

Before you begin, please make sure your pup gets enough physical and mental exercise each day. We must meet our dogs' daily needs if we expect them to calmly learn new things.

Step One

First, break the old jumping cycle so you can instill new habits. In other words, prevent all jumping up on people from now on. Here's how:

- Configure your space so your pup is behind a baby gate when you enter rooms so that he can no longer rehearse jumping on you in greeting.

- Alternative: toss a few tidbits behind your puppy as you enter (to give you a moment to enter and squat down low or cue a sit to pre-empt the jumping).

- When visitors arrive, keep your puppy behind a baby gate or on a leash until he is calm enough to accept treats held at knee-level. It helps if your company has a chance to come in and have a seat first. If you have a tiny dog, just hold him in your arms before you open the door and he has a chance to run toward visitors.

- Keep all arrivals extremely low-key; no speaking, no attention (these are rewards) until the pup is calm.

- Use an indoor, lightweight dragline for a week or two for very energetic jumpers. Step on it while you are interacting with your pup (it should have just enough slack to allow him to stand or sit without any tension on the line). Should he launch himself, it will seem to him like gravity is super powerful and he will not be able to complete the action. (But it won't hurt him because the pressure from the flat buckle collar will be on the back of his neck; try it with your own arm acting as the dog's neck and you'll see what I mean.)

Step Two

Meantime, teach a new action to replace the jumping up, like "sit." A dog cannot jump up and sit at the same time. Therefore, every time your puppy approaches you, don't wait to see what he's going to do. Rather, immediately ask him to sit, then reward with a treat and calm attention. Do this each time you interact with your pup. Once he sees that sitting earns your attention, he'll offer it just as enthusiastically as he used to offer jumping up. (This won't work if the humans unwittingly continue to reward the jumping up, so be very aware of your own tendency to touch, speak to, look at, and coo at your pup when he puts his paws on you. Even if he's very, very cute.)

Avoid this common trap: do not wait for your pup to jump on you, and then cue him to sit. By doing so, you are actually encouraging the jumping by following it with a rewarding interaction. Should your pooch somehow skip the sitting part and jump up, abruptly turn away. Then wait. The moment his rear hits the floor, quickly face him again and calmly praise him (but do not feed a treat). Do not rely on this back up plan as your main strategy, however, or you will be stuck with the behavior chain of jumping-turning your back-sitting for all your days on the earth. Instead, be prepared to preemptively cue and reward the sit each time your puppy approaches you, so the jumping up never makes an appearance. That way jumping will disappear and you will be left with polite sitting in its place forever more!

Step Three

Finally, if you reward your pup's new habit of sitting to solicit an interaction with you, then sit will become the new default behavior:

In order for sitting to become your pup's new default behavior, it is your job to reward him each time he sits. Have your dog sit before he gets everything he wants, including human attention. Simply cue your dog to sit and reward by releasing him to any of the following activities (plus any others that your puppy loves):

- Meals and treats
- Outdoor time
- Having the leash put on
- A chance to come out of the crate
- A chance to come out of the car
- Games like fetch or tug
- Access to anything he loves (dog friends, belly rubs, furniture, the yard)
- Attention and affection

FAQ's On Rewarding Sit Rather Than Jumping

"What if he jumps up while we're working on the plan?"

Say nothing (avoid words like "off" or the pup's name, and scolding words like "uh-oh" as all of these provide the reward of attention) and immediately turn your back. Gravity will lower your dog to the floor. When all four paws are on the floor, face your pup and offer low-key praise. Prevention (by cuing the sit or crouching low to greet your pup) is the faster, more effective route. Be quicker to cue the sit or crouch low so jumping doesn't occur.

"Will this work with visitors to the house?"

All visitors must be in on the plan. For fastest results, enlist the help of a couple of friends for a few intensive sessions. Keep your pup on leash. Skip the doorbell at first and just have your friend enter. When your pup sits on your cue, visitor #1 may briefly pet, calmly and slowly. If your puppy sits, quickly reach in and feed him a treat to make his behavior extra rewarding for him. Alternatively, you may release the pup to approach the person, provided your helper is prepared to feed treats one at a time at knee-level (or lower). If your pup jumps, say nothing. You will have already instructed the helper to abruptly turn their back (and step out of your pup's reach) in response to jumping up. They will face the pup for petting as soon as he sits. They should pretend to arrive over and over (five times would be good) so the puppy rehearses oodles of sitting for rewards and attention. Then repeat with visitor #2. Finally, you should invite everyone to have a slice of cake to thank them for their trouble.

Your helpers can pretend to be strangers out on the street as well, to present the opportunity to reward the puppy for sitting when you run into friends on a walk. Be prepared with very special treats to reward your pup for sitting in such a challenging setting. Be quick to release him to approach the person after you reward (the person should crouch low, and even feed treats below their knee-level to reward for all paws staying on the ground). The sequence of Sit-Treat-Release-Approach is a great habit to teach right off the bat.

You can also help your pup succeed by teaching him what to do once he is released to greet you or others. For example, if you teach your pup to touch his nose to people's shoes or to their palms, you can release from the sit and then cue one of those. Or just hand everyone some treats to feed at their knee level for the next few weeks (keep a container by your front door). Or sprinkle treats on the ground for him to hoover up. The pup will be busy with his task while the person pets him. Then be quick to encourage the pup back to you so he is not tempted to jump on the person. Aim for short, successful sessions.

"Will this stop the puppy from pawing at us?"

Dogs often paw at us for attention when we're seated. To solve this you can use a similar technique as for jumping up; simply ask for a sit as your pup approaches you. This allows you to create a rewardable moment, and rewards build good habits. Calmly pet the dog under the chin and praise quietly. Should he raise a paw, remove your hand & turn away. Should he escalate the pawing, say nothing and leave the room for at least ten seconds. If you are consistent, your dog will learn that sitting quietly earns him your affection, but that pawing you causes you to leave.

The Animal Game

This is a terrific game to teach your kids (and their friends) to play with your puppy (obviously always under your supervision). Or, if you have a high threshold for embarrassment, play it with your puppy yourself. It teaches dynamite self-control on everyone's part, it will make you laugh, and it makes teaching stay into something you'll actually want to practice. Your pup will learn to take wacky kid behavior in stride. Plus, a puppy engaged in a sit-stay, even with weird or exciting stuff going on, cannot jump on anyone.

What you need: sit on cue (see the Sit section), super tasty treats, a quick review of the Ten Secrets of the Pros, and the imagination to act out a few animals. For pups new to this, let them wear a dragline that you can step on if needed to prevent jumping in a moment of puppy exuberance.

Step One

Have your child choose an animal and decide what movements and sounds he will use to act out his animal. Explain that you will coach the animal to act sleepy, scared, happy, or fast. Sometimes you will cue the animal to make sounds that are soft, medium or loud. Each of these variables represents an additional challenging distraction for your puppy.

 If your child or puppy will need help keeping calm or quiet, assign animals like bunny, seahorse, or fish. When your pup is ready for a big challenge, choose monkey, frog or pony. It can be helpful to practice ahead of time with your child and without the puppy.

Step Two

Cue your puppy to sit. Ask your animal helper to act out a quiet, sleepy version of the animal off to the side while you stay in front of the puppy. Reward the puppy for any and all ear flicks, head turns or glances that indicate he is noticing your child and still staying put. Just pop a treat in his mouth lickity split (no need to say anything, which might confuse your child or delay your treat delivery).

Step Three

After 3-5 seconds of that, release the pup and have your child choose a second animal (step on your pup's line and engage him in low-key play with a rope toy for this brief down time).

Keep the game to five minutes total. Increase difficulty by tweaking your child's movement or sound, one variable at a time. Your child can also gradually move to the other side of the pup, in front of him and eventually all the way around him. Should the pup get up before you've released, as usual do not reward. Ask your child to make the animal he is portraying freeze in place. Then wait a moment and your puppy will likely sit. When he does, do not reward with a treat (we don't want sit to mean "sit then get up then sit again"), calmly praise him, cue some sleepy movement from the animal, and then reward your pup with a treat. Release. Build up duration of sitting and degree of animal wildness separately and very gradually, as you don't want the pup constantly over challenged and rehearsing failure by getting up out of position. It is important to rehearse and reward success.

I highly recommend letting kids (who are ready) treat the puppy for staying while you pretend to be an animal. You can also play this game in locations where jumping has been a challenge, such as where guests come in to your house or where the pup is fed.

Bold or Bashful?

Bold Puppy Tip: Sometimes, in a very over excited state, your bold puppy may not only jump up, but also clasp his front legs around your leg in an attempt to mount your leg. Because this can be a rewarding activity for your pup, and rewards cause strong habits to form, I recommend interrupting this action by calmly and silently taking your pup by the collar and removing him, in a steady, gentle, sideways motion. Once he is off your leg, maintain your hold on the collar to prevent him from starting the cycle all over again. Just wait. Once he has calmed down (but not beforehand), do not merely release his collar, but rather engage him in another activity like some training, a walk, or a game like find it or fetch. Make note of what circumstances trigger this behavior so that you can give him an alternative game to play *before* he even has a chance to jump on your leg. Most pups abandon this behavior if you pre-empt and interrupt it consistently.

Bashful Puppy Tip: It can be overwhelming for a bashful puppy to sit still while tall, looming humans lean over to pet them. Consider giving your pup an alternative, like showing off a trick. It also works well to teach them to target open hands with their nose. That way you can reward the sit, and then release the puppy to nose-bop a stranger's hand or cue the puppy to turn away from the person and bop your hand.

Chapter 25

Teach Your Pup To Come Running To You When You Call

No dog can resist a good game. In fact, being distracted by a game (like keep away, scent tracking, or tag with dog friends) is usually the reason our puppies may not come when we call them. The perfect solution is to make coming to you the best game of all! It works, and it's fun. Work up to playing these games (use a lightweight long line) where you may one day need great responsiveness from your dog should he get loose: just outside your front door or gate, at the park, in the woods along your favorite trails, and in your neighborhood.

We interrupt this promising training session for a reality check: your puppy is not a robot who will come with 100% reliability his whole life (beware of fast-talking salespeople who may claim otherwise). I'll bet at some point someone has called you and you have not jumped up and raced toward him or her, even if you could smell dinner aromas wafting through the air. That doesn't mean you don't think they are worth listening to. And it should go without saying that none of us should have to jump to attention out of fear of consequences for a slow response. Nobody's perfect, including the best-trained dog. Keep your puppy safe by using a leash in public spaces (it's usually the law) and near traffic. Use a fenced-in area for off-leash time (a physical fence, not something that could hurt or scare him like a shock fence. Besides, only a physical fence will keep him confined if he is motivated by what's on the other side, and will keep other animals and people out).

Ok, back to making coming when called a fun game. For starters, practice good habits and avoid common pitfalls during this early training phase:

- Call your puppy only when you are prepared to deliver extra special rewards (make them a surprise, not a bribe).

- Never call your pup for something she considers unpleasant, like putting the leash on to end a play date, getting her indoors, giving a bath, or scolding.

- Never scold your dog for coming, even if she just dug up your garden, chewed your shoe, or bolted out of the yard. Prevent these to begin with by using a fence, a leash, a crate, and dog-proofed confinement areas like a baby-gated kitchen.

- If she jumps up while playing these games do not ask her for a boring sit or turn your back. Your #1 priority is to reward coming to you, and if you don't she will soon think coming is lame and avoid it. Instead, set her up to succeed. To prevent jumping up as your pup approaches, simply squat down before she reaches you and reward, or hold your hands at your knees as you reward.

- If you need her near you to bring her inside, confine her or give her a bath, go get her rather than call, or she will learn to associate coming when called with bad consequences.

Alrighty, let the games begin!

Start indoors and work your way outside where there are more distractions. Only play these games for as long as your puppy is dying for more (5 minutes max).

Gotcha Game

This teaches your puppy to love the most important part of coming when called, being caught by the collar. Put five treats in one hand

and use your other hand to grasp your dog's collar (you'll feed one treat for each grab). Keep the treat hand still by your side until you can feel the collar in your other hand. Grab the collar close to your body, feed one treat. Make sure you grab first, pause (treat hand still by your side), and then feed. Repeat. Play indoors and out. Your puppy should start to love seeing your hand reach out to grab him. If not, use more fantastic treats, or make it easier by just lightly touching or even just pointing at the collar.

Opposites Attract

Have a helper squat down and hold your pup by his chest or by the collar. When they push the pup back gently away from you, your puppy will be inclined to do the opposite, which is lean towards you. When you call, your helper should release their grasp on the pup, who will burst forward to catch up to you. Whoop it up, run away, and praise when the puppy catches up to you. Turn and reward down low to prevent leaping and biting.

Hide-n-Seek

A helper holds your pup. You sneak off and hide (on tip-toe and dramatically glancing back over your shoulder as you leave the pup). You then yell, "Buster, find me!" The helper releases the pup. Cheer and feed treats close to your body (like your knees) once your dog finds you. Make it easy at first until he gets the idea; first hide in the same room behind a chair, then try another room. If you don't have a helper, toss a treat away from you to get a head start while your dog goes after the treat.

Ricochet Recall

Two or three helpers stand about 20 ft. apart, all are holding special treats. Take turns saying, "Fifi, here!" then cheer wildly. If she hesitates *even for a moment*, take off cheering in the opposite direction and she should come bounding after you. Feed favorite treats when she arrives. Then briefly hold the collar and withdraw your attention (so you won't seem so interesting). Release the collar when the next person calls and cheers the dog over to them.

Chase Game

In a fenced-in yard, take off running! When your dog catches up to you, praise and reward with treats. Then take off in another direction. Be unpredictable! Never, ever chase your dog; that's a great way to ruin your come-when-called (can you guess why?).

Sit-Zoom-Sit

Play the chase game as above, but add in the element of self-control so your pup learns to listen carefully to you even if he's feeling super wound up. As your pup catches up to you, turn to face him and cue him to sit. Reward with a treat, release, and zoom away! Repeat. If he is so excited he can't sit, don't repeat the word. Give him a moment to calm down (just wait quietly). He will likely sit. Reward by releasing and inviting more running, rewarding with actual treats only when he sits instantly. You may also need to build the excitement gradually, by walking at first, or running not quite so far or so fast.

Chapter 26

Down On Cue

Here's a quick weekend project for you: teach your pup to lie down on cue. Teaching down on cue is just like teaching the sit, in that when you catch your puppy going into the down position of his own accord, you reward with a luscious treat. It's pretty easy to predict when he will choose that position if you observe your pup's favorite resting spots and sleepy times of day. After a handful of repetitions of being rewarded the moment he lies down, your puppy will begin lying down on purpose in order to earn a treat (imagine if someone gave you $50 every time you happened to tuck your hair behind your ear; in short order you would start tucking your hair back on purpose to get that $50). The more it is the puppy's idea, the stronger and more reliable will be the result.

The key action you need to reward is when his elbows hit the floor (meaning he's all the way down). Feed a treat between his front legs (this strengthens understanding of what's being rewarded, because the pup ducks his chin to take the treat and his center of gravity shifts slightly back and even more "down"). If you like you can say "good!" or "yes," but really, the most important thing is to be quick about delivering the treat the second the elbows hit the deck.

Just put a handful of (quite luscious) treats in your pocket first thing in the morning and reward him every time he lies down, and after a day or two he'll start lying down in order to get you to feed him a treat. When you're willing to bet your car he's about to do so, say "down" one time only, wait, and when he does it reward like bananas with treats between his front paws. Do that for another few days and you'll notice the time shrink to nothing between when you say "down" and when he assumes the position.

Remember to release him from position each time with "ok" otherwise having it on cue will be fairly useless to you (because he'll just hop right back up). Reward him for staying in position two or three seconds longer at a time, followed by a clear release of "ok," and you'll be on your way to down-stay. Fancy schmancy!

A slippery floor helps when you are looking for downs because it will be easier for your pup to slide down. Otherwise just be alert for times he is likely to lie down and be ready with your treat delivery. It is also very helpful to look at the spot on the floor you want your puppy's chest to land rather than looking into his eyes.

If you are in an extreme hurry and want your pup to lie down in one day instead of two, or if your pup is so active he never lies down on his own, you can use a tantalizing treat on a slippery floor to shamelessly bribe him into position by gradually lowering the goodie to the floor (especially easy from a sit or by you sitting on the floor and drawing the treat under one raised knee so the pup has to practically crawl under your knee to follow the treat). Only do that two or three times, so that you are not faced with the headache of fading the treat, your arm movement and your body position out of the picture. Get the ball rolling by slowly lowering the treat straight down to the floor, but for subsequent repetitions just wait, staring at the floor, and from then on only reward in the down position rather than bribing. Have faith, it really works!

Chapter 28

Go To Your Place: A Simple Solution To A Zillion Problem Behaviors

Imagine how cool and useful it would be if you taught your puppy that when you say, "Spot," it means he should lie down and relax on his spot. If your puppy has a portable spot he can go to on cue, you won't have to deal with your dog doing any of the following:

- Sampling appetizers or snacks off your coffee table
- Hanging around the dinner table or under your baby's high chair
- Putting paws on the counter while you prepare a meal
- Being a drama queen while you prepare his meal
- Gobbling up something that has been dropped
- Distracting your kids while they are doing their homework
- Bothering guests while they are seated or standing
- Going berserk when someone rings the doorbell
- Pestering other pets in your household
- Nudging you or dropping toys in your lap while you try to relax after a hard day of earning money to buy dog treats
- Jumping up on people you meet on the street
- Straining and whining at other dogs or people in the veterinarian's waiting room or puppy class
- Getting over-stimulated and ignoring you in dog training class

None of those things can happen if your dog is lying quietly on a mat. Your dog will benefit because he will earn plenty of rewards in the form of praise, petting, treats, a stuffed Kong, and a chance to chill out.

This is not advanced training. It's the kind of useful, basic skill like sit or come that any dog can and should learn. It is also easy peasy for you to teach. It looks fancy, like a cupcake you might find only in a New York City bakery. But it is so straightforward to teach that anyone can do it. More like a cake mix right out of the box (but you don't have to tell anyone our little secret).

If your dog is named Spot, I'd recommend calling this action something like "Place." Please take a moment to visualize what would happen otherwise. It's amusing.

Goal: You say, "Spot," and your puppy responds by trotting over to his spot, lying down and staying there (relaxed) until you release him with "ok."

What you need: A bath mat or portable accent rug available to your pup only during training sessions (not a dog bed or towel), a handful of soft, non-crumbly treats that are extra special, an indoor location free of distractions. Some practice with teaching "down." Oh, and your puppy. Use a leash if your pup is easily distracted and wanders off.

How to teach: Train in 5-minute sessions.

Session One

Spread out the mat and then sit or stand no more than two feet from the mat. Look at it. Be immediately ready to notice your pup out of the corner of your eye. When he looks or merely glances at what you're looking at, say, "yes!" and bowl a treat onto the mat for him to eat (this is not bribery because you are rewarding the act of looking at the mat, not tossing the treat in order to get the puppy to look). When he is finished eating, encourage him off the mat by patting your leg and backing up. Repeat 2-3 times.

Now, the hardest part of this training is that the human must resist the urge to hint, coax, lure and entice the puppy to look at the mat by pointing, leaning, or outright bribing with food. If you do this, the training will take ninety-two times longer, because the puppy will just be focused on your shenanigans and not work it out for himself. Just stand there and look at the mat. It's painful, but I know you can do it.

Session Two

Warm up with the above exercise. After your pup does the "I am looking at the mat because I figured out that makes cookies appear," routine a few times, let him eat his reward off the mat, then count to yourself one-banana, say "yes," and feed him another treat on the mat. He just went to his spot and stayed there for one second. Woo hoo! Now anything is possible! Repeat a few times, encouraging him off the mat in between repetitions.

For your next rep, allow your pup to look at the mat, but don't say a word. Just wait. His wheels will turn and he will walk over to the mat. When even one of his paws touches it, say "yes!" and feed him a treat. On each subsequent repetition, withhold your reward until another paw touches the mat (such that by the fourth repetition, he is leaving you, walking up to the mat, then putting all four paws on it). That means he is a genius. (If he seems super tentative, you can reward each paw touching 2-3 times before holding out for another paw touching the mat.)

Session Three

Start right where you left off. Spread out the mat and wait. Your pup will look at it, walk to it, and stand on it. Reward as usual. On the next repetition, count to two bananas and then reward.

Take a short break and play with a toy, or just run around the room and act silly together.

Back to training. Go near the mat. Wait. After he is standing on it, wait some more. He will very likely plop his butt into a sit, because by now he's figured out from your other training that sitting pays the big bucks, and that staying on the mat is also highly rewarding. Say "yes" like you won the lottery and feed him several treats like it's a big deal (which it is!).

Only do a few of those because ultimately we really want him to lie down, right?

Session Four

Hopefully you've taught your pup to lie down on cue at some other point during the day. If you haven't done that introduction to "down," go ahead and do that first. It'll just make everything go that much smoother and faster.

Once your "down" practice is going well, break out the portable mat again. Repeat the last exercise, except this time wait for a down position. Stare at the spot you want those elbows to land, so that you don't stare at your puppy and distract him. When he goes even partway into the down position, lavish him with praise and treats fed low between his front legs. Remember to release with "ok" before he has a chance to hop up.

Final Sessions

Now we make it look like real life. For the next few sessions, try setting up in several different places in the room. Then try your body in several different positions (sitting on the floor, in a chair, or lying on the couch (good practice for when you have the flu and don't want the puppy smothering you). Work up to different rooms in the house and you standing at varying distances from the mat. Use awesome treats. If you get stuck at any point, try again, but do make it a wee bit easier if you get two failed attempts. Remember, sessions are still under 5 minutes.

What's that, you want to know if you should be saying "Spot?" No, you are not saying "Spot" yet, because we do not want him thinking that a so-so version is what you want when you use the magic word. You want "Spot" to mean the whole enchilada! So, patience please.

When you can roll out the mat, in any room of your house, with you sitting or standing, from any distance you like, and your pup trots right on over to the mat and lies down, waiting for your release before he gets up (after a few seconds), then you are ready to add the magic word. Just say it right as he's about to do it. You can even make a game out of it, restraining him by the collar and then cueing "spot." When you let go, he may just run full tilt to get to his place!

You can add to the length of time he is able to stay there by counting more bananas before you feed his low-down treat. After you get to 10 seconds, you can likely add time in 3-5 second increments. Always throw in a super easy, short one rather than continuously just asking for more and more duration. I highly recommend working on this while you watch Dancing with the Stars, or, you know, the Nightly Business Report, so you can get in a lot of rewards for lying quietly and extend the duration, all in the environment you're likeliest to need it.

If he's getting up a bunch before you release him, he is informing you that you need to do a better job of explaining what will earn him the reward. In other words, feed more treats more frequently when he's doing what you want. He is a baby and he needs your help, so help him by rewarding generously so he'll know what to do more of. Soon he'll be lying there for 30 minutes at a pop while you have cocktails with your friends, and you'll long for the days when he was so young and naïve, all cute and eager to learn this new trick. (I had a client who had worked up to 20 minutes. She asked her pup to go to his spot, forgot to release him, and when she got home from the store he was still there, all alert, 45 minutes later! She felt bad, but really I think it gave him a chance to show off.)

Some Real Life Variations To Work Up To

Leaving Human Food Alone

This process teaches your dog that human food being set out is a cue for him to move away from it and relax on his spot. Put a plate with no food on it on the coffee table. Cue your dog to go to his spot. Reward your pup for staying on his spot. Repeat with a bland food item on the plate, like a banana still in its peel, then with increasingly tempting food items at subsequent training sessions. Always reward your dog generously for staying put. Remove the plate before you release your pup.

Curing Doorbell Madness

Put the mat at the end of the entryway near the front door and cue "spot." Knock on the wall. Reward! And then knock on the door from the inside. If that is easy, play a doorbell sound on your smart phone, louder and louder until you can just ring the real doorbell. Each time you up the ante, cue "spot" and reward like bananas. Your dog may even start running to his spot when he hears the doorbell!

Calm Around Guests

Introduce staying on his spot despite other distractions, like people walking in and out of the room. Increase difficulty only gradually. Start with a family member who's been around all evening casually walking in without talking to him, working gradually up to the hardest challenge: someone who's just gotten home who smiles at your pup as they enter the room. Reward like bananas.

Spot On The Road

Use a smaller and smaller size mat, until you have a washcloth-sized mat (or an actual washcloth) that you can take on the road. Now you can ask your dog to go to his washcloth spot at a café, the veterinary waiting room, your kids' soccer game, or just outside the kitchen while you are whipping up a meal.

Spot For Life

After a couple of months the spot will be so rewarding that you can rely more on praise and petting to reward his efforts. Do surprise him with treats now and then, especially for a really challenging situation. Reward him especially generously for scenarios that you don't have much chance to practice, like seeing a neighbor on the street, puppy class, or trips to the vet. Or even better...set those scenarios up with helpers, and in short order you'll have the world's best behaved dog!

Part V

The Tail End: As Your Puppy Becomes An Adolescent

Chapter 29

How To Help Your Puppy Blossom Into A Great Dog

Most teenagers, regardless of their species, go through a challenging transition as they make their way to maturity. In other words, teenagers can be a real pain in the behind. And so it will likely be with your puppy. Just when you're getting the hang of things and seeing fantastic results, at around 6 months of age his behavior may start to aggravate you, yet he won't be quite as fuzzy and cute any more. His hearing may appear to become selective. His energy levels may spike. He may chew up one of your possessions seemingly out of the blue.

The thing to remember is that you have laid an excellent foundation that still resides inside that teenaged brain. Follow a few simple guidelines and you should get through doggie adolescence relatively unscathed.

1.   Increase the amount of daily aerobic exercise your pooch gets. You may need to hire or barter with someone, but it's essential to meet his growing exercise needs for your sanity and to give your pup a fair chance to behave well. Avoid dog parks. Instead, offer truly aerobic exercise like additional 20-30 minute walks, swimming, or hikes through the woods. Any of these could be shared with a favorite dog buddy. Double check with your vet to make sure the activity you've chosen promotes healthy growth.

2.   Maintain routines. Keep regular mealtimes and offer micro training sessions throughout the day. For

example, cue your dog to sit, nose touch or down before you release him with "ok" out the door, gate or car.

3.   Be vigilant about providing plenty of authorized chew opportunities. Feed meals as food puzzles and rotate edible chew items like Sam's Yams and marrow bones. Your dog's teeth will be adult-sized by the time he is 10 months old, and may irritate him in the final stretch of this development. This often prompts a spike in chewing activity.

4.   Continue to provide socialization opportunities with dogs, people and experiences that will feature prominently in the rest of your dog's life. Like a middle school social mixer, this can be both fun and awkward, so be prepared to help your teenager with a nose touch, games you take on the road, and taking a step back when needed. This is no time to be shy about getting help from a professional dog trainer if you see a troubling behavior more than once. (See the When to Get Help section.)

5.   Offer your dog more freedom in the house once he's both housetrained and you're past his chewing phase (it all comes together at around a year of age). Make this change at a glacial speed. Choose a puppy-proofed room or two to baby gate rather than letting him loose in the entire house. Provide him with an engrossing "coloring book" like a stuffed Kong or Busy Buddy toy, then go take a shower. If that goes well, provide the same set up and run a 30-minute errand. Take your time with this process and always give him something more interesting to do than develop bad habits like barking out the window or engaging in interior design projects like putting a hole in your rug.

    If you prefer your pooch not get on the furniture, provide a plush dog bed on the floor and spread cookie sheets on the couch in your absence. Unlike other approaches, this won't frighten or hurt him, but frankly it's not that inviting an option to lie on a metal sheet, so your dog will likely avoid hopping up. You can always just spread a washable blanket on the couch and call it a day. Unless your dog is aggressive about guarding the furniture from you, it is fine to share it and, despite the myths, cannot in itself cause other problems.

6.   Brush up on your training so you can keep communication sharp between you and your teenager:
   - Teach a new trick each month (like shake, roll over or sit pretty)
   - Call and generously reward your dog at least once a day to keep coming when called sharp
   - Enroll in a fun class. You can work toward a doggie BA, MA or PhD via the Canine Life and Social Skills (C.L.A.S.S.) program, or choose a tricks or agility class

7.   Last but not least, continue to observe your growing dog so that you can harness the power of real-life rewards. Experiment with the following as his preferences may shift as he develops:
   - Treats (home made, chopped up leftovers, dog treats from the farmer's market)
   - Toys (squeaky, bouncy, flying disc, fleece tug, treat dispensing)
   - Praise (soothing, high pitched and goofy, a favorite phrase, a song)
   - Petting (slow under chin, behind ears, gentle circular motion on main muscles)
   - Attention and interaction (catch him doing something right and offer long strokes down the back, a smile, gentle praise)
   - Action (chasing after you, come when called games, a new activity like swimming, homemade agility course, sand digging pit with treats hidden in it)
   - Goodall Games to identify your dog's favorite activities

- Cue to "go sniff" as a reward for lovely leash walking

- Cue to "say hello" to greet a person or dog to reward a sit-stay or focus on you

What other everyday pleasures are important to your dog that you can use as rewards?

Teach Your Dog. Let Your Dog Teach You.

If anyone had any idea about the amount of time, effort, tears, confusion, sleep deprivation, frustration and family stress that raising a puppy involves, no one would do it. But you have jumped in, and you have survived! I bet you are doing a better job than you think you are.

I hope you have found tips in this guide that make your journey more enjoyable. You won't get everything right. It's okay. I don't, either. It's one of the best gifts dogs give us. They let us make mistakes, we learn, and we try to do better next time. Puppies help us grow and they show us how to handle a challenge. They can be like mirrors, except a lot less judgmental, more forgiving, and a lot more fun.

Try to spend a little bit of time each day, or even once a week to start, appreciating your puppy. What do you like about her? What is her cutest feature? What has she been the quickest at learning? She will help you slow down, be grateful for what is going well, and give you back, in joy and companionship, all the effort you have put in a thousand fold.